Sojourning in a University Academic Vineyard

Sojourning in a University Academic Vineyard

A Reflection on Teaching, Research, Service and Collegiality

Allyson A. Sesay, Ph.D.

SOJOURNING IN A UNIVERSITY ACADEMIC VINEYARD
A REFLECTION ON TEACHING, RESEARCH, SERVICE AND COLLEGIALITY

iUniverse books may be ordered through booksellers or by contacting:

iUniverse
1663 Liberty Drive
Bloomington, IN 47403
www.iuniverse.com
1-800-Authors (1-800-288-4677)

Because of the dynamic nature of the Internet, any web addresses or links contained in this book may have changed since publication and may no longer be valid. The views expressed in this work are solely those of the author and do not necessarily reflect the views of the publisher, and the publisher hereby disclaims any responsibility for them.

Any people depicted in stock imagery provided by Thinkstock are models, and such images are being used for illustrative purposes only. Certain stock imagery © Thinkstock.

ISBN: 978-1-4917-5545-7 (sc)
ISBN: 978-1-4917-5546-4 (e)

Print information available on the last page.

iUniverse rev. date: 12/07/2015

CONTENTS

INTRODUCTION

ACADEMIC ADVISING

MULTICULTURALISM/MULTICULTURAL EDUCATION

NOTES OF APPRECIATION

CONCLUSION

DEDICATION

This book is dedicated to the many students I had the opportunity and pleasure to teach and advise at Shaw University during my 15 years of sojourning; also, to the many colleagues I got to know and fellowship with during my tenure.

ACKNOWLEDGMENT

I want to take this opportunity to express a special appreciation to my wife, Irene, for her love, understanding and unwavering support to me during the course of my 15-year sojourning at Shaw University, as well as during the times spent away from her company while putting this work together.

Thanks also to Mr. Marco S. Conteh for the design of the beautiful cover of the book.

PREFACE

This work is written as a way of documenting and sharing the story of my 15-year sojourning at an institution where I had worked for the longest number of years in my professional career in higher education. My 8-year service at UmanuDanfodio University, formerly the University of Sokoto, in Sokoto State, Nigeria provided me a variety of rich academic, cultural and personal experiences that have contributed immensely to enhancing my professional growth.

I was going to put down my Sokoto, and Nigeria experiences in a book like this one but circumstances, including a fire accident that gutted my residence in Sokoto, did not make this possible. My rare socio-cultural experiences as the only black faculty member at the two universities where I worked in the state of Maine for three years also presented me with an opportunity for a book of this nature. However, for one reason or the other, this did not materialize. Determined to not let this happen with my 15-year experiences at Shaw University in the state of North Carolina, USA, the impetus for writing this book remained very strong as I dedicated myself into preparing this manuscript amidst many competing projects.

This work which I have titled *Sojourning in a University's Academic Vineyard* chronicles my experiences and contributions in academe as a teacher, researcher, academic adviser, community servant, and colleague. The studies reported in the book have focused primarily on two broad areas – academic advising and multiculturalism/multicultural education. These are critically important areas with far-reaching implications for providing a good quality education for the students placed in our care to develop into the critical-thinking, problem-solving, and social-change agents needed to function effectively in our increasingly interconnected and interdependent global village.

I must add that I am grateful to have had the opportunity to acquire a wealth of rich professional and personal experiences while sojourning at a great institution with a very rich history and a laudable mission, and which has made great contributions to education to not only the State of North Carolina, but to the United State of America and the world at large. I am happy and lucky to have been a small part of that history.

CHAPTER 1

Introduction to Shaw University

A brief introduction to Shaw University will provide a background to facilitate a better understanding of the topics discussed in this book. The university, a church-related, co-educational, liberal arts institution, founded in 1865, is the oldest historically black higher education institution in the Southern United States of America. Its mission is "to advance knowledge, facilitate student learning and achievement, to enhance the spiritual and ethical values of its students, and to transform a community of diverse learners into future global leaders" (Shaw University, 2010, p.2). The education so provided will enable the graduates to "lead productive lives and to pursue successful professional careers as citizens in a globally competitive society" (p.2). Though the university seeks to attract students of diverse backgrounds, "it has maintained a special interest in the education of minorities who have been traditionally excluded from the mainstream of American education" (Shaw University, 1997, p.4). The university provides instruction at both the undergraduate and graduate levels. Apart from being the oldest historically Black university in the South, Shaw University possesses other characteristics of historical significance. For example, it built the first dormitory for Black women in the United States, named Estey Hall, which is listed in the National Register of Historic Places; it founded the first four-year medical school in the country which in 1886 graduated its first medical doctors. Graduates of Shaw's medical school provided selfless services to their communities. In the political realm, Shaw University conducted a study that investigated the problem relating to the exclusion of deserving Black World War II veterans from the distinguished Medal of Honor for their heroic service. The study culminated in the award of this honor to seven of the ten recommended veterans, which was undeniably a great achievement for the veterans and also for justice.

Another achievement of political significance was the establishment of the Student Non-violent Coordinating Committee (SNCC). Started in a very small way by four students who decided to organize a sit-in in Greensboro, North Carolina to protest racial injustice, the SNCC grew into a major grassroots organization that adopted the non-violent direct action philosophy and style advocated by the civil rights champion, Dr. Martin Luther King, Jr. Formed in 1961 at a meeting held on Shaw University's campus, the SNCC has been characterized as the civil rights movement's "cutting edge." http://www.sncc.50thanniversary.org/sncc Putting their lives on the line and, for some, their educational careers on hold for some time, members of the SNCC worked relentlessly to enhance voter registration which culminated in the election to political office of a number of prominent black officials across the southern United States of America. It is safe to say that the election of our first Black president in the person of Barrack Obama can be attributed to some extent to the uncompromising and selfless activities of the SNCC which was launched at this historic higher education institution, the first in the South, called Shaw University. No wonder, therefore, that the SNCC saw it fitting to hold the 50th Anniversary of its founding at Shaw University in April of 2011.

Student enrollment, as of the fall semester of 2011-2012, was 2,550, according to statistics from the Office of Strategic Planning Institutional Advancement and Evaluation (OSPIRE). Of this population, 34.5 percent of the university's students were enrolled in the College of Adult and Professional Education (CAPE) at nine locations across the state of North Carolina and two correctional centers. The CAPE programs were designed specifically to provide educational opportunities for working adult (non-traditional) students by offering classes in the evenings and on Saturdays.

The Divinity School had taken the lead in offering online courses at the university. Online course offerings to supplement the Video Tele-Conferencing (VTC) course delivery system were introduced in 2006 at the undergraduate level, starting in the Department of Education, to meet the needs of Education Majors and other students at distant locations. The technology for online course delivery has changed from Blackboard to Moodle.

The university's student population remains predominantly African American (about 85 %). The population of White, non-Hispanic students has remained very low – 1.20 percent in the 2006-2007 academic year to 1.80 percent in 2010-2011(OSPIRE, 2011, p. 51). Asians/Pacific Islanders, Hispanics/Latinos, and Native Americans together made up less than one percent of the entire undergraduate student population in the fall semester of the 2010-2011 academic year. The university has to do more to increase its students' racial/ethnic diversity. Representation of Whites and other non-Blacks among the full-time instructional faculty was somewhat higher. In the fall semester of 2010-2011 academic year, Whites accounted for 25 percent of this group (a 7 percent increase from 2006-2007), Asians/Pacific Islanders made up seven percent, Hispanics two percent, and Native Americans one percent.

As a religious institution which was founded by an ordained Baptist minister, Shaw University places great emphasis on inculcating religious values in its students. Character education has therefore been an important and integral part of the institution's curriculum and has been institutionalized starting with Freshmen Orientation. "All freshmen are required to sign the following code of conduct:

- To hold in trust the traditions, practices and laws that govern this historic institution.
- To respect all property, discouraging vandalism, and theft of any and all things that do not belong to me. Most especially, to respect

myself, exhibiting virtues, morals, discipline and the cultural matrix upon which Shaw University was founded.

- To be accountable always for my personal, social, and professional conduct.
- To celebrate diversity: I recognize, and therefore, affirm the dignity and worth of others who live, work, and/or study in the community.
- To discourage any behavior within myself or among my peers that will jeopardize the integrity and reputation of this university.
- To foster an open caring environment" (Shaw University, 2008, p.24).

With the arrival in 1988 of President Dr. Talbert O. Shaw, an ordained minister with a doctorate in Theological Ethics, the focus on character took on greater dimension. Predicated on his belief that "the moral drift in our nation, that has invaded college campuses, thus impacting student behavior in many ways," he championed the move to revise the institution's curriculum requiring all students, regardless of their majors, to take nine credit hours of ethics and values "… beginning with introduction to the discipline of ethics and advancing to courses dealing with professional ethics" (p. 25). Though this requirement has been modified during a recent re-visioning of the university's curriculum to provide greater emphasis on improving students' reading and writing ability, ethics, nonetheless, continues to be an important component of a Shaw University student's education.

A unique aspect of Shaw University that epitomizes its genuine concern about and commitment to cultural diversity is the presence of a mosque which serves persons of the Islamic faith in the institution and its community. A mosque conspicuously located in a Christian university like Shaw is not common in the United States of America. Since I have been at this Baptist-affiliated university over the past 14 years, I have never heard of or witnessed any form of religious discrimination or intolerance, not even after the disastrous terrorist attacks of September 11, 2001 in New York and Pennsylvania by Muslims that caused the deaths of thousands of innocent Americans, including children.

The university has faced some challenges during its 146 years of existence mainly because of poor finances, but it has managed to survive and has continued to produce quality graduates, many of whom have made and continue to make significant contributions to the nation and the world. Table 1.1 below summarizes, in chronological order, the accomplishments of just a handful of the many distinguished alumni of this historic institution.

Table 1.1: Accomplishments of Selected Shaw University Alumni

Alumni	Year Graduated	Notable Accomplishment
John O. Cosby	1881	1st. President of A and M College, now North Carolina A and T State University.
Lula C. Fleming (Native of Mpalaba, SW Africa)	1885 (Estey Seminary)	Returned to Africa (the Congo) and became the 1st colored female missionary there.
Peter W. Moore	1887	1st President of Elizabeth City State College, now Elizabeth City State University, North Carolina.
Angie E. Brooks	1949	Assistant Secretary of State; Associate Justice of the Supreme Court of Liberia, West Africa; President of the United Nations General Assembly in 1970.
James E. Cheek	1955	First Shaw University alumnus to become president of the institution (1963-1969). Appointed at the age of 30, he was the institution's youngest president.
Edward C. Dolby	1966	President, Bank of America Carolinas

William L. Pollard	1967	Current President, Medgar Evers College, Brooklyn, New York; former President, University of the District of Columbia, Washington, DC.
Willie E. Gary	1971	Multi-millionaire; philanthropist; started his own law firm in 1975; now senior partner of a nationally renowned law firm; current Chairman of Shaw University's Board of Trustees.
James "Bonecrusher" Smith	1975	First college graduate heavyweight boxer.
Shirley Caesar	1984	"Queen of Gospel Music"; renowned Minister; Grammy Award Winner.

Source of Data: Adapted from Shaw University's Fact Book (12th Edition). 2010-2111.

Shaw University laid the foundation for the establishment of other colleges in the state of North Carolina. As can be seen in the table, examples of these institutions are North Carolina A & T State College which became the present North Carolina A & T State University; and Elizabeth City State College, now Elizabeth City State University. The first presidents of both these institutions were Shaw University alumni. Other alumni have also made significant contributions in the field of higher education administration. Dr. James E. Cheek, a 1955 graduate, became Shaw University's first alumnus to be appointed president of the institution. The main library, the James E. Cheek Library, was named in his honor. After a successful tenure as President of the University of the District of Columbia in Washington, DC, 1967 graduate William L. Pollard took over the presidency of Medgar Evers College, a position he still holds.

This historically Black institution, founded specifically to provide education for freed slaves, has also produced many graduates from Africa who returned to their native countries and made significant contributions to their development. Two such prominent alumni are Angie Brooks who not only served her native Liberia as Associate Justice of the nation's Supreme Court but also served as President of the United Nations General Assembly. After receiving her degree in theology from Shaw's Estey Seminary, Lula Fleming returned to Africa where she became the first Black female missionary.

The university's alumni have also made important contributions in the fields of business, entertainment and sports. Edward C. Dolby of the class of 1966 rose to the prestigious position of President of Bank of America Carolinas; the legendary Shirley Caesar, Grammy Award winner, dubbed "Queen of Gospel Music," is not only a great musical success but also a renowned minister. The sport of boxing has not been known to have athletes who have had some college education, let alone college degrees. Shaw University alumnus of the class of 1975, James "Bonecrusher" Smith, was an exception; he was the first heavyweight boxer to graduate from college with an earned, and not an honorary degree.

A 1971 graduate, Willie E. Gary, is a special success story. Coming from an impoverished economic background, the kind of background from which I believe founder Elijah Shaw envisioned the students he targeted would come, the resilient Willie Gary entered Shaw University on a football scholarship. Other colleges and universities did not give him a chance for a postsecondary education. After graduation from Shaw University, this highly self-motivated and resilient young man went on and earned a law degree from North Carolina Central University. Shortly after he established his own law firm which did not take long to metamorphose into one of the most successful firms in the United States, and I am inclined to believe, one of the best in the world. A senior partner of this prestigious firm, Attorney Gary has employed some of the best legal minds from the best law schools in the nation. The firm has won several high-profile cases, gaining as much as five hundred to seven hundred million dollars in each settlement. This multi-millionaire and philanthropist, has never forgotten Shaw University's contribution in making him the success he is today. He is the current chairman of the institution's Board of

Trustees, and he continues to support his alma mater financially, morally, and spiritually. Attorney Gary exemplifies the fact that any student coming to Shaw University can become successful in life, if he or she is provided the encouragement and support to build a strong self-concept and develop his or her potential to the fullest extent. It has to be emphasized, however, that the students have to play their own part and take responsibility for their own education. Success does not come through luck but hard work and perseverance. This is my unwavering belief and my commitment to my work to help students succeed here at Shaw and in life afterwards. Those with the right attitude and work ethic have been able to achieve excellent outcomes. Upon graduation from Shaw University, many of them have gone on to earn their master's and doctoral degrees in various disciplines including the sciences, education, political science, business, and law from some of the best universities in the nation.

Though not adequately compensated financially, Shaw University's faculty, several of whom are alumni with terminal degrees from some of the nation's renowned universities, are nevertheless committed to carrying out their duties and responsibilities to help the institution achieve its mission and goals. They continue to excel in their tripartite functions (i.e., teaching, research and service) as members of the academy. For example, two faculty members (of whom I am proud to be one) have won the prestigious Fulbright Fellowship. Several faculty members have won very competitive national research grants bringing in huge sums of money that have helped and continue to help the institution to enhance its academic programs as well as to provide services to its community. Major grant winners in this regard include Dr. Ademola Ejire whose research has focused mainly on environmental and health problems; Dr. Daniel Howard, former Director of the university's Institute for Health, Social, and Community Research, with a major focus on eliminating, or at least minimizing health disparities among ethnic groups in the university's community and beyond; Dr. Elvira Williams and her team on Nanoscience and Nanotechnology; Dr. Highsmith's research in the area of botany; Dr. Sharma's work on improving science education; Dr. Joan Barrax's work on improving parents' involvement in their children's education; Dr. Mercy Fapajuwo's work on enhancing faculty members' ability in the use of instructional technology in their work. It must be remarked that these scholars won their grants in keen competitions with other scholars from major research institutions nationwide. These and other achievements have helped the university maintain its viability as a sound and healthy place to nurture future leaders and empower the citizenry for the nation's development and that of our global village.

Twice since I have been here, the university has successfully gone through the rigorous re-affirmation of accreditation exercises by the Southern Association of Colleges and Schools (SACS); both the undergraduate and graduate programs in education are accredited by the National Council for the Accreditation of Teacher Education (NCATE) and the North Carolina Department of Public Instruction (NCDPI); the Department of Allied Health's programs in Athletic Training and that in Kinesiotherapy are nationally accredited by the Commission on Accreditation of Athletic Training Education (CAATE) and the Commission on Accreditation of Allied Health Education Programs (CAAHEP), respectively; and the Social Work program is also nationally accredited by the Council of Social Work Education (CSWE). The university is currently preparing for its re-affirmation of accreditation visit by SACS in 2013.

The Way Forward

As the American society becomes increasingly culturally diverse and our world more interconnected and interrelated, the need for our educational institutions, from K – 16, to prepare our students to be able to function effectively and competitively as individuals as well as citizens of this global village becomes critically important. Those of us in the teacher preparation field, for example, ought to take due cognizance of these national and global realities as we educate the teachers into whose hands the education of our children and youths (our future leaders) will be entrusted. Schools of the 21st century need teachers who are reflective practitioners, critical-thinkers, problem-solvers, and leaders who utilize the findings of research of their own and of other researchers to improve their job performance. It must be emphasized that the work of teachers at all levels is becoming increasingly complex and highly demanding of their mental, physical, and emotional capacities. At all levels of the educational system, teachers must deal with challenges such as the student population explosion (including those with various types of disabilities), an expanding student-teacher ratio, coupled with barely adequate infrastructural and instructional resources, decreasing funds for education, and a breakdown in social structures, including the family. Little wonder why the burnout and exodus of teachers, especially the brightest ones, continue to plague our nation.

Some folks, including educators, have wondered whether public education in the country will survive the 21st century. While I do not share this level of pessimism, I do believe that the education system as a whole faces colossal problems that need to be addressed with all seriousness and sincerity by all– that is, the government at the federal, state and local levels, the private sector, parents, teachers, administrators, and the community at large. The education of our students from economically disadvantaged backgrounds in the urban as well as suburban and rural areas is particularly in peril, given the current state of our national and global economy. The 2013 revolts involving the destruction of property and looting by the youths in London and here in the United States are clear manifestations of the grave national consequences of frustration due to an inadequate education, unemployment, and poverty.

Education is the key to solving many of our societal problems, such as the kinds of youth problems mentioned above. The need, for example, for teachers who not only possess a sound knowledge of the content areas of their disciplines but who also possess the professional dispositions including a commitment to making a difference in their students' lives cannot be overemphasized. John Ruskin, as quoted by Johnson, et al. (2010), was quite right when he said, "Education is a painful, continual, and difficult work to be done by kindness, by watching, by warning, by precept, and by praise, but above all – by love" (p. 358). Producing and, also importantly, retaining these kinds of teachers at all levels (K-16), who are academically qualified, dedicated, and empathetic is a very ambitious goal. Nevertheless, it can be achieved with the financial and moral support from all stakeholders and beneficiaries of the education enterprise including the government at all levels and agents in the private sectors. In this colossal task of education, we cannot overlook the critical role and cooperation of the non-academic staff in providing and maintaining an atmosphere conducive to the proper nurturing of our students for the world of work and also for life.

CHAPTER 2

Academic Advising at Shaw University: What Students Think

Introduction

Academic advising is a critical and integral component of any college or university educational program. There is abundant research evidence showing a positive relationship between good advising and students' persistence and graduation (John Gardner, 1995). It is, therefore, very important that an institution periodically evaluates its advisement program in order to determine how well it is serving its students and to utilize the results of such an evaluation to improve the program. It is against this backdrop that this study was conceived and conducted. The study explored the perspectives of a cross-section of students on the quality of academic advisement being provided them.

Procedure

A survey methodology was adopted for the study. I designed a structured questionnaire which I used for data collection. The instrument contained evaluative questions and statements about the academic advisors and the students themselves. A copy of the questionnaire is provided in Appendix A. A total of 700 questionnaires were administered to the students in group settings in which faculty members administered the questionnaires in their classes. The completed questionnaires were returned to me immediately after their administration. This manner of administration was deemed important so as to prevent the students from discussing the questions, and thereby, influencing each other's responses. The goal was to obtain each student's independent perspective and a collection of perspectives as diverse as possible. A total of 520 fully completed questionnaires were returned, reflecting a response rate of 74 percent. Characteristics of the sample are presented in Table 2.0.

Participants/Sample

The sample for the study consisted of 520 randomly selected students from across the university including the CAPE locations. This number represented 18% of the university's undergraduate student population. The study was limited to undergraduate students. As can be seen from Table2.1, the majority of them (26.5%) were from the Department of Business and Public Administration, followed by Social Sciences (21.2 %). Teacher Education and Natural Science and Mathematics represented 11.5% and 11.2%, respectfully. The other departments accounted for less than 10% each of the sample. Regarding classification by year in college, the majority of the students were juniors (28.1%) and seniors (25%). Gender-wise, females accounted for 61 percent of the sample. Off-campus residents made up about 50 percent. Traditional and non-traditional students accounted for 55.2 percent and 43.8 percent, respectively.

Table 2.1: Characteristics of the Sample.

Characteristic	F	%
Major		
Business & Pub. Admin.	138	26.5
Social Science	110	21.2
Education	60	11.5

Natural Science & Math	58	11.2
Religion & Philosophy	46	8.8
Allied Health	38	7.3
Computer & Info. Science	24	4.6
Mass Communication	22	4.2
Humanities	12	2.3
Visual & Performing Arts	10	1.9
Undecided	2	0.4
Total	520	100.00%
Classification		
Freshman	114	21.9
Sophomore	112	21.5
Junior	146	28.1
Senior	130	25.0
Other	18	3.5
Total	520	100.00%
Gender		
Male	190	36.5
Female	330	63.5
Total	520	100.00%
Residence Status		
On-Campus	216	41.5
Off- Campus (Non-Cape)	94	18.1
Off- Campus (Cape)	210	40.4
Student Type		
Traditional	287	55.2
Non-Traditional	228	43.8
No Response	5	1.0
Total	**520**	**100.00%**

The pre-coded questionnaires were analyzed using descriptive statistics consisting of frequency, and percentage responses to the questions raised were calculated and the results presented in tabular form. Also, verbatim quotations of the students' responses to some of the open-ended questions were sorted and used to elaborate on some key issues raised in the study. The results are presented in the next section.

Findings

The findings of the study are presented and discussed under the following headings: students' perception of academic advising, students' self-evaluation, students' assessment of their advisors (qualities they liked and those they disliked about their advisors), recommendation of their advisors to others, and students' suggestions to improve advisement.

Students' Perception of Academic Advising

Without a proper understanding of what academic advising really involves, it would be difficult to devise an appropriate advising system that would effectively address issues and problems that may have an impact on students' chances of achieving academic success and professional success after graduation. My first concern, therefore, was to explore the students' understanding of academic advisement. As shown in Figure 2.1, the responses indicated that over 50 percent reflected a rather narrow perception of academic advising: As many as 39 percent perceived academic advising as limited to helping students register for classes or limited to matters directly related to a student's program and not with those matters of a personal nature or concern (13.9%). This narrow perception of academic advising is what experts in the field refer to as the 1960s view (Habley, 2003). This view limits the process of academic advising to helping students to choose courses and register for classes. However, a sizeable percent (45%) of the responses suggested that the students had a broader perspective of academic advising. This contemporary perspective encourages advisors to take cognizance of students' personal goals and life experiences as well as to guide them towards a career choice and preparation for graduate school. For example, one student remarked about her academic advisor as follows: "She does not know about any of my personal accomplishments outside the Department." This student went further to express her views thus:

If she [her advisor] shows some interest in my overall well-being, I'd feel comfortable enough to talk to her about more than just advisement. To me, the advisor should serve as a mentor as well. If advised correctly, the advisee should be with that advisor for four years.

Figure 2.1: Students' Perception of Academic Advising

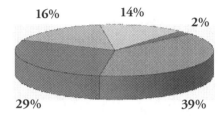

Helping students to choose their courses and ensure that they register for the right courses each semester.

It should involve helping students with career choices and preparation for graduate school.

It should involve advising/counseling on personal matters affecting the student.

It should be limited to matters directly related to a student's academic program such as course selection and graduation requirements and not with personal problems.

Other

There can be no denying that personal matters, such as those relating to work, finance, relationships, and childcare, among others, can have important impacts on a student's academic performance, persistence, and graduation. For example, academically weak students who hold a 40-hours-a-week job would need some specific, deliberate advice on how to balance work and academics and how to set their priority regarding work and school. Retention data from OSPIRE (2010) have shown that the major reasons why students drop out of the institution relate to personal, non-academic problems.

Students' Self-Evaluation

Since academic advising involves collaboration between advisors and advisees, I was interested in finding out how the students evaluated themselves as participants in the advising process. They were required to indicate whether they strongly agreed, agreed, disagreed, or strongly disagreed with some salient statements pertaining to their responsibilities as advisees. They could also indicate if the statements were not applicable to them. The results are presented in Figure 2.2.

Figure 2.2: Students' Self-Evaluation of Their Role in the Advisement Process

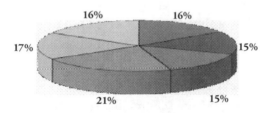

- ▨ I make and keep appointments with my advisor
- ▩ I come to my advising session prepared (e.g. courses pre-selected, proper forms)
- ▨ I strive to clarify my personal values and goals with my advisor
- ▨ I accept responsibility for my academic choices and monitor my progress toward graduation
- ▨ I have a long range academic plan that outlines the courses I still need to take
- ▢ I retain the courses my advisor and I select during advisement sessions and make changes only after consultation with him/her.

Analysis of the students' responses showed that 70 percent of those who responded indicated that they either strongly agreed or agreed that they made and kept appointments with their advisors. Thirty-seven percent of them strongly agreed that they went to their advising sessions prepared, such as having pre-selected their courses. Another 40 percent agreed that they did likewise. A sizeable percentage of them either strongly agreed (36%) or agreed (29%) that they had long-range academic plans that outlined the courses they still needed to take. Thirty-six percent strongly agreed that they strove to clarify their personal values and goals with their advisors, and 38 percent agreed. It was also important and interesting to find out that the vast majority of the students (91%) reported that they accepted responsibility for the academic choices they made for monitoring their progress toward graduation.

The university requires that students first be advised before registering for any class. An advisement form for this purpose is available, and both advisor and advisee sign agreeing on the courses that they had both selected for registration. Regarding this matter, most of the students reported that they either strongly agreed (41%) or agreed (38%) that they adhered to the courses they and their advisors had selected and that they made changes only after consultation with their advisors. There have been some cases in which students had changed their course schedule without prior approval by their advisors, and this had led to their taking courses they did not really need, and consequently, delaying their progress toward graduation. In fact, this study also revealed that 15 percent of the students indicated that they strongly disagreed or disagreed that they adhered to the course schedule they and their advisors had agreed upon during their advisement session. Adhering strictly to the advisement contract between advisors and advisees cannot be overemphasized.

Students' Assessment of Their Advisors

It was important to find out what the students thought of their advisors regarding their handling of the advisement process. Again, the students were presented with several statements relating to some key qualities and practices of an academic advisor. They were to indicate whether they strongly agreed (SA), agreed (A), disagreed (D), or strongly disagreed (SD), with each of the statements, or if they were not applicable (NA). Candid reflections on such statements would provide invaluable feedback for advisors' self-evaluations and plans to utilize such feedback to improve advisement.

The results of the analysis of the students' responses are presented in Table 3. There was general agreement (44% strongly agreed and 31% agreed) that their advisors were friendly, approachable, and genuinely concerned about them. Though 19 percent of them strongly agreed and 24 percent agreed that their advisors kept in contact with them by e-mail, and a phone, a note or in person, a significant number of them either disagreed (24%) or strongly disagreed (21%) with this statement. However, there was general agreement among the students in the following areas: that their advisors kept regular hours and were adequately available, were concerned about their overall welfare, spent sufficient time discussing their circumstances, and had a thorough knowledge of the requirements in their majors. However, as can be seen in Table 2.1, there were some problem areas of concern to advisors in particular and to the university in general. These included the following: Not enough information and encouragement from advisors to help students take in a timely manner professional examinations, such as the Praxis tests, LSAT, GMAT, and internal examinations such as the English and Mathematics Competency Examinations required for graduation; insufficient information about campus resources (e.g., the Academic Assessment and Achievement Center, the Curriculum and Materials Center, the Career Development Office, the Counseling Center) and extra-curricular activities; inadequate provision of information pertaining to career/internship opportunities in students' areas of interest; seeking students out when they are having academic difficulties, such as low mid-term grades and excessive class absences. These concerns, which are in congruence with the comprehensive perception of academic advising described earlier, are critical to enhancing the academic advisement system, and consequently, to improving students' retention and graduation.

Table 2.2: Students' Assessment of Their Advisors

Statement about the Advisor	Responses				
	SA	A	D	SD	NA
Is friendly, courteous, and demonstrates a genuine concern for me.	111	78	20	10	34

Keeps in contact with me via E-mail, phone, note or in person.	49	61	60	54	30
Keeps regular office hours and is adequately available.	69	93	35	25	32
Is concerned about my overall welfare – personal and academic.	72	90	39	21	31
Allows sufficient time to discuss my circumstance.	74	84	29	22	34
Has a thorough knowledge of the general core requirements of Shaw University.	96	95	20	11	32
Has both a current and thorough knowledge of the requirements in my major.	105	94	17	9	28
Explains professional exams (e.g. Praxis, LSAT, and GMAT) to me and encourages me to take them as early as possible.	45	66	61	28	58
Continually reminds me to take the mathematics and English Competency Examinations as early as possible.	33	59	61	36	59
Identifies potential obstacles to meeting educational goals and discusses viable options.	52	73	49	27	45
Offers information about campus resources(e.g., Triple A, CMC), extra-curricular activities, etc.	43	64	52	32	57

Provides information on career/internships opportunities in my area(s) of interest or refers me to the Career Center.	53	64	41	33	57
Seeks me out when I am having academic difficulties (e.g., excessive class absence, low mid-term grades)	39	59	32	37	63
Overall, I am generally satisfied with my academic advisor and his/her advising.	76	83	36	32	23
Overall, I am generally satisfied with the system of advising in my Department.	61	93	39	36	19

❖ **SA = Strongly Agreed, A = Agree, D = Disagree, SD = Strongly Disagree, NA = Not Applicable**

When asked whether they were, overall, generally satisfied with their advisors and the quality of their advisement, most of the students, 30 percent, reported that they strongly agreed and another 33 percent agreed. With regard to advisement in their departments, 62 percent of them indicated that they were generally satisfied with the system of advising. However, a sizeable percent expressed dissatisfaction in this regard – 30 percent disagreeing and 14 percent strongly disagreeing. A more detailed report of results based on departmental comparisons is presented later in this chapter.

The results discussed above, as noted earlier, are based on the students' responses to a number of closed-ended questions, which I pre-determined. The students were also provided the opportunity to express their perspectives and feelings freely about their advisors and the system of advising in their departments by responding to some open-ended questions. They were required to mention qualities they liked and those they did not like about their advisors completely and as honestly as they could. Box 2.1A and 2.1B show an assortment of their responses in this regard.

Box 2.1A: Qualities Students Liked About Their Academic Advisors

Qualities They Liked
• She knows about requirements dealing with the university requirements and the Education Department.
• Nice when it's something not dealing with the Education Dept.
• He is available at any time and sends me e-mails of events that I need to attend because of my major.
• I like everything. She's Peace.
• He listens and tries to find a solution to every problem. He cares what's going on in my school career.
• She is a good listener.
• My academic advisor sincerely seems to understand my desire to go back to college.
• She is very caring and generally concerned with my well-being and all aspects of my life.
• His expertise in mathematics; making sure I'm ready academically for certain math classes Dr. --- [I withhold name] is always available during his office hours and stops whatever he is doing to help me or advise me.
• My academic advisor is very punctual. Her door is always open and she gives excellent advisement to what is best for me rather than rushing to get me out of her office.
• He wants to make sure that I graduate on time & succeed.
• I really don't know who my academic advisor is but I have been acquiring information from Dr. … and he has given me good advice about my studies. He is very thorough and if he does not know, he will find out about it and get back to me within a reasonable time.
• Trustworthy, easy to talk to, caring of each student.
• My advisor helps me to stay on track.
• A friendly attitude.
• She is neat, keeps appointments; I can talk to her about anything. She keeps me updated (always informative) and tries to keep me focused. She knows her stuff.
• Friendly; seems to want to help.

- She is very friendly and ever ready to help.
- She is down to earth and very approachable.
- Telling me the truth.
- She follows the rules of the academic advisement process. She shows concern for my grades. When I am with her, I have her full attention.
- She keeps me on top of things that I would normally let pass me by or forget about completely.
- She seems to be very knowledgeable of what she is talking about, and she is patient with me, which is good.
- Knowledge of required courses, interest in my future.
- Academic Advisor has been different for every semester, but they have all been professional and knowledgeable.
- I like everything about her except there's not enough of her to go around.
- I wish there were more Mrs. X.
- A good role model - one who knows education and is concerned.

The names of advisors whom the students mentioned in the quotations listed in the table above were deliberately omitted, regardless of whether such quotations were positive or negative. The intent of the survey was not to identify specific "good" and "poor" advisors, but to generate helpful information to improve advisement in the university. The students mentioned several good qualities in describing their advisors: knowledgeable of program requirements, helpful, friendly, and caring. On the negative side, which should be of greater concern to us in our efforts to improve advising, many of the students' responses centered around advisors' attitude (e.g., bossy, impatient, lack of concern for their students' situation outside the classroom), and not much attention given to students at the CAPE sites. See Table 2.1B for details.

Box 2.1B: Qualities Students Did Not Like About Their Academic Advisors

Qualities They Did Not Like
• My advisor acts as if she rarely has time for her students, she may make an appointment, write it down, and forget about it. She seems to have an attitude every time I see her, and tries to rush through the advisement.
• Doesn't seem to want to hear my opinion on my class schedule; just signs me up for classes. Not really easy to talk to.
• He seems not interested in my future plans. He just helps me make my present schedule and does not give me any encouragement at all.
• Gives wrong information. Arrogant attitude.
• Easily frustrated.
• The one quality I did not like was that she seemed unfamiliar with the courses that I needed to take for my major. She seemed a little unsure of what my best course schedule should be.
• She can be rude and controlling sometimes. She is not always understanding.
• They [advisors] don't understand that sometimes we don't want to take classes at a certain time.
• My department chair had me take a course which I didn't belong in [need]. I took all the pre-requisites at my community college prior to coming here. He also didn't check my transcripts, and he needs to be dealt with accordingly.
• Not returning calls. I fully understand that the advisors are busy; however, not being able to go to them directly is a problem, so returning calls is important.
• A little too quiet.
• She blows things out of proportion.
• I have no idea about my advisor's qualities. I have yet to meet her. I am very disappointed with this area of my education. I have not been advised about the courses I should or should not be taking and at the end of the semester I'm learning that some of my current classes should not have been taken at the same time which is why I am not doing well in either class.

- Doesn't seem to know what she's doing; she is too busy most of the time. Doesn't seem to have a clue about advising me as to what I need to take or sit down and go over what I already have. I need and have been asking for a new advisor.
- I believe that Shaw has a good education program but as a non-CAPE student attending a Shaw CAPE Center I feel much neglected.
- She doesn't agree with any of my personal goals. She doesn't call or get in contact with me at all. I make all appointments. She doesn't know about any of my personal accomplishments outside of the Department.
- She is never in her office or never even there at the given appointment time.
- The only thing that I do not like is that sometimes I don't feel as though I get the same respect that other students get.
- [Does not] Separate personal feelings and business. My advisor has not been very professional.
- Bossy and too busy to talk.

Recommendation of Advisors to a Relative or Friend

Academic advisors who are good and effective are very likely to be recommended to other students by their advisees. Based on this premise, I posed the following question: "Would you recommend your advisor to a friend or relative?" Analysis of their responses revealed that as many as 65 percent of them would do so. Twenty-eight percent of them, however, said they would not make such a recommendation. The rest of them (7%) indicated that they were not sure whether or not they would make such a recommendation. This is a cause for concern.

When asked why they would or would not recommend their advisors, their responses were similar to those given in response to the questions on the qualities they liked and those they disliked about their advisors, as shown in Table 4.0, namely, they would recommend their advisors because they were approachable, helpful, knowledgeable about their program of study and interested in their personal well-being. Reasons why they would not recommend their advisors revolved around their advisors' attitude toward the advisement process, a lack of professionalism, and lack of a genuine concern about their interests and problems, outside of choice of courses and registration for classes.

Students' Suggestions to Improve Academic Advisement

In addition to giving the students an opportunity to express their views on the quality of advisement in their departments, they were also asked to provide some suggestions on how to improve the system of advisement. For the most part their suggestions bordered on matters having to do with a change of attitude by their advisors. They preferred advisors who were more approachable and interested in their general welfare, not just in helping them with registration for classes. This situation speaks directly to the broader and current definition of academic advisement in contrast to the narrow 1960s definition described earlier. The following are quotations of their suggestions to address their main concerns:

- The advisor [should] have a better attitude and be more encouraging.
- [The advisors should] take more time to see what's best for the students.
- The advisors should become more interested in my life and give me information about programs.
- The advisors should keep my needs in mind when planning my schedule.
- I expect my advisor to inform me about new trends in my area.
- When the advisors come to the CAPE Centers, there should be an education advisor that travels with them as well. (Cape students felt neglected.)
- The advisors should be more informed about my future goals or expectations.
- Could the advisors at least acknowledge that they know we exist by emailing us 1st [at the beginning] of the semester or by mid-term?
- I want my advisor to contact me when changes are made in the department and not at the last minute.

- It should be helpful for me to have my own copy of the Handbook [Department's Handbook] so that I can refer to it as needed.
- The advisors should provide more assistance with transfer credits.
- The main campus needs to be timelier about posting funds and academic credit transfers. It took almost a year to post what courses transferred.
- As a student at the Ashville CAPE, I think the idea of using the Director as a student advisor as well as using instructors physically located at the center is an excellent idea. (They know the students very well).

Summary, Suggestions, and Conclusion

Summary

The purpose of this study was to explore the views of students regarding the system of advisement provided at the university. By providing the students an opportunity to evaluate the system, the university would be able to generate important information that would be used to revamp the system and to improve the quality of advisement. Consequently, it is anticipated that this would help to enhance students' achievement, retention and graduation, which, as noted earlier in this report, positively correlate with good academic advising.

By means of a structured questionnaire the data for the study was collected. A total of 520 students took part in the study. The questionnaires were administered to the students in group settings in their classes. Analysis of the data revealed salient information critical to enhancing the quality of advising provided in the various departments of the university. The students, overall, were satisfied with the quality of advising provided them. They reported positively about their advisors' knowledge of the requirements of their programs and of relevant departmental policies, and their readiness and willingness to help them. Important concerns and problems they reported included the following: advisors not taking enough time to discuss their problems, especially non-academic problems, unprofessional attitude and disposition, such as being harsh and disrespectful, frequent change of advisors, not enough information and encouragement to take professional exams (LSAT, GMAT, GRE, PRAXIS, etc.) to enter their careers or graduate school, and insufficient information about campus resources, internship and career opportunities.

This study also revealed that some advisors appear to hold to a 1960s definition of academic advising, that "the task of academic advising is concentrated in the opening days of registration and enrollment and consists of aiding students in the selection of courses" (Asa Knowles, as quoted by Wes Habley (2003, p.26). This may explain, at least in part, why some students complained about their advisors not being interested in their personal, non-academic problems and concerns that may directly or indirectly impact their academic well-being. Reflecting on the two landmark publications by Crookston (1972) and O'Banion (1972), which contributed to the development of an expanded definition of academic advising, Wes Habley (2000) points out that "...advising was far too critical to be defined as a perfunctory, clerical function that involves only the prescriptive selection and scheduling of courses" (p.35). David Crocket, as quoted by Habley (2003), presents the broader view that "academic advising assists students to realize the maximum educational benefits available to them and helps them to better understand themselves and to learn to use the resources of the institutions to meet their needs" (p.26).

It is obvious that to function effectively as an academic advisor who espouses and practices the contemporary conception of academic advising described above, it would require much more than helping students to choose courses and register for classes. It will require, among other things, that the role of the academic advisor be extended beyond the classroom and his or her office. Research has shown that the most important and memorable academic experiences of students are those that occur outside the classroom. For example, a 2001 study by Harvard University professor, Richard Light, as reported by Thomas Brown (2003), indicates that when students were asked to "think of a specific incident or moment that had changed them profoundly," four-fifths of them reported an incident or situation that occurred outside the classroom. Also, it has been shown that "institutions which consciously reach out to establish personal bonds among students, faculty, and staff, and which emphasize frequent and rewarding contacts outside the classroom are those which most successfully retain students" (Tito, 1993), as cited by Brown. If an institution does not focus on this way to increase retention, is there insufficient understanding of this broader, more comprehensive definition of academic advising? Or is there an unwillingness to make the greater effort that would be required? These questions ought to be addressed and will be addressed in a later study.

Suggestions

Based on the findings of this study the following suggestions are offered to help enhance the departments' efforts to improve academic advising. Advisors should

- adopt the contemporary and broader conception of academic advising and put it into practice;
- have professional attitudes and dispositions at all times, for example, treating all students (traditional and non-traditional, CAPE and non-CAPE) with respect;
- acquire a thorough understanding of each program's requirements as well as relevant departmental and university policies.
- attend to students' non-academic concerns or problems. If nothing else, they should listen and show a genuine concern about their advisees' situation;
- exercise patience in dealing with students and be prepared to go to the greatest possible extent to help them; and
- get to know their advisees better by developing friendly but appropriate relationships with them.
- The departments should
- minimize, as much as possible, the switching of advisees from one advisor to another during the course of the students' stay at the university.
- Keep students at the CAPE sites abreast of activities and developments in departments of the university;

- hold regular meetings with advisors and advisees at least twice a semester; and
- share and exchange views and concerns. They should highlight positive accomplishments by students, faculty, and departments and not just discuss problem cases.

Students' Responsibility

Successful academic advisement is achieved when all parties concerned (faculty, administrators, staff, and students) contribute their fair share. Academic advisement is not meant to spoon-feed students and allow them to become dependent but rather to guide them to become mature and responsible adults who can take independent decisions and ready to bear the consequences of such decisions. Against this backdrop I offer the following suggestions to students to help them enhance their success:

- Know your program (major) very well – its requirements such as
  - ➢ the departmental core, required, and elective courses

- Know your departmental policies such as
  - ➢ requirements for graduation
  - ➢ transition points/progression through the program (e.g. GPA requirements, external exam needed at various stages)
  - ➢ internship requirements
  - ➢ discipline policies (e.g., classroom decorum, dress code, plagiarism, etc.)
  - ➢ class attendance
  - ➢ repeating a course
  - ➢ etc.

- Know university policies such as
  - ➢ academic progress/standing/probation and dismissal
  - ➢ credit hours for major and minor
  - ➢ graduation requirements – total credit hours/GPA; removal of "I" grade

- Get to know at last one faulty member very well a year. Also, get to know other members of the university (e.g. from the registry, admissions, counseling, health services, work study, finance, etc.). Develop and maintain a network of advisors and friends. **Remember, it takes the whole university village to effectively advise a student.**

- Know your **program checklist** very well!
  - ➢ At the end of each semester enter your grade for each course on your checklist and check them off. In this way you can keep track of courses you have completed and those to be taken.
  - ➢ Go through your checklist with your advisor to make sure the entries in yours match those in the checklist your advisor keeps in your folder in her office. By so doing mistakes, omissions, inconsistencies, etc., can be spotted in advance and corrected. We as advisors are not perfect. We can and do make mistakes, some of which can have serious consequences on your future. For example, a delay for one semester can mean a lost opportunity for a great job or advanced study opportunity. Take charge of your future!

Conclusion

Academic advising is too important a university function to be treated lightly. Kramer (2003) points out that "other than teaching, no other college activity seems to enjoy more legitimacy than academic advising" (p.1). A number of research studies have shown "a significant correlation between quality advising, student satisfaction, and enhanced persistence and graduation" Gardner (1995). It is therefore critically important for the departments to bolster their efforts to improve this important aspect of the academic life of their students. The psychic income or personal satisfaction to be derived by advisors for providing good advising cannot be overemphasized. The appointment in 2003 of a Coordinator of Academic Advising by the Department of Education – the first such position in the university's history – is a very positive step to enhance this crucial function. It is a move which other departments across the university should seriously

31

consider. The various departments could then work collaboratively with the newly established Academic Advisement Center to improve academic advising in the university.

It is hoped that the findings of this study will help inform better policies and actions to help improve academic advisement at the university. In this regard, an undergraduate participant in a survey focusing on the Department of Education which I conducted in 2004 recommends the following: "Study this survey and take note of points made" (p.13). By paying close attention to self-evaluation of our practice, we can begin to appreciate the impact we make on our students' lives as they go through college as well as after graduation.

Finally, academic advising, in its comprehensive sense, and as revealed in the findings from this study, is demanding of advisor's time, knowledge, patience, and understanding. Academic advising is, in fact, a form of teaching (Kramer, 2003). This invaluable aspect of a faculty's work must therefore be well recognized andappropriately compensated. Academic advising should be an important criterion in the evaluation of faculty performance and should be rewarded accordingly.

References

Brown, T. (2003). *Advice that matters. What do students hear and remember?* Paper presented at the 2003 NACADA National Conference, Dallas, Texas.

Crockett, D. in Wes Habley (2003). Realizing the potential of academic advising. NACADA Summer Institute, St. Charles, Illinois.

Gardner, J. (1995). In Tom Brown (2003)

Habley, W. (2003). *Realizing the potential of academic advising. NACADA* Summer Institute, St. Charles, Illinois.

Habley, W. *Current practices in academic advising.* Gorgon, V.N., Habley, W. and Associates (2000). *Academic advising: A comprehensive handbook.* San Francisco: Jossey-Bass.

Kramer, G.L. (2003). *Advising as teaching.* In Kramer (Ed.) *Faculty advising examined: Enhancing the potential of college faculty as advisors.* Bolton, MA: Anker Publishing Company, Inc.

Light, R. (2001). *Making the most of college. Students speak their minds.* Cambridge: MA: Harvard University Press.

Sesay, A.A. (2004). Report on a Study of Students' Perspectives on Academic Advising in the Department of Education at Shaw University, Raleigh, North Carolina.

Tinto, V. (1993). *Leaving college: Rethinking the causes and cures of student attrition* (2nd ed.). Chicago. IL: University of Chicago Press.

CHAPTER 3

Balancing the Demands of Athletics and Academics: Experiences of Shaw University Student-Athletes

Introduction

When perceived as a comprehensive university function, academic advising is concerned with "assisting students to realize the maximum educational benefits available to them to better understand themselves and to learn to use the resources of the institution to meet their special educational needs" (Crocket, 2003). Though one may argue that all students have certain predetermined needs and special characteristics that require specific attention from their academic advisors or from the college's advising system, the point can be justifiably made that there are some student populations that "deserve special academic accommodations and advising services in order to maximize their potential for success" (Ender and Wilkie, 2000, p. 118). Examples of such special populations include students with disabilities; gay, lesbian, and bisexual students; and students with exceptionally high academic abilities, as well as underprepared or developmental student learners, and student-athletes. This chapter is based on a study I conducted that focused attention on student-athletes, a group that deserves some special attention because of the tremendous task they face to meet the demands of their athletic programs on the one hand and those of their academic programs on the other. There is tremendous pressure on the student-athlete to strike and maintain this balance successfully. Speaking about this pressure, Lanter (2006) writes: "The pressures to succeed academically and athletically are enormous for college athletes. The pressure comes from themselves as well as parents, peers, and coaches" (p.1). Explaining the situation of the student-athlete, Curry (1999) writes:

> Student athletes practice a minimum of twenty hours per week (By-Law NCAA* Manual), usually year round. Most devote even more when you add film time. Their non-athlete peers obviously have much more time to devote to academic matter (i.e., studying, professorial office visits, career seminars, etc.) p.162.

It is important, therefore, that the institution provides easy access to services. For example, student-athletes are, by definition, doubly in need of resources to help them stay healthy and make the right choices regarding nutrition and drugs.

The pressure created by this task of trying to balance athletics and academics is one some faculty do not fully understand or even care to understand and appreciate owing in part to stereotypic and negative perceptions of the student-athlete. As an instructor who has had many athletes in his courses over the years, and also as a parent of two former student-athletes, I fully understand and appreciate the student-athletes' peculiar situation of striving to achieve success in both their athletic and academic pursuits. It is critical for advisors to take due cognizance of the fact that special populations, such as student-athletes, have characteristics and advising needs that are different from those of other students on campus. Such an

---

*   National Collegiate Athletics Association

understanding is invaluable for developing a congenial academic advising relationship, a desideratum for effective advisement and students' success.

In comparing student-athletes with their non-athlete counterparts, Walter and Smith (1989) identified at least four unique differences between these two categories of students, differences that academic advisors should take cognizance of in order to fully understand the life and lifestyle of an intercollegiate athlete. The differences are as follows:

1. Issues of time and energy devoted to their sports. Most sports "require a commitment of at least three hours a day, five to six days a week, fifty-two weeks a year."
2. Lower grades earned in high school. Due to the fact that some student-athletes come to college with significantly lower high school grades and standardized test scores (e.g., SAT), they have to work a lot harder than their peers in order to succeed academically.
3. Frequent travel to compete off campus resulting in student-athletes missing class more than other students.
4. A lifestyle that often involves living in a fish-bowl-type atmosphere. Because of student-athletes' high visibility on campus and throughout the community, Walter and Smith noted, "their behavior is often far more scrutinized and magnified than the behavior of other students." On account of the pressure this fish-bowl-type lifestyle creates, some athletes, the authors noted, "may resort to unproductive social behaviors or substance abuse" (p.329).

The combined effects of the four factors mentioned above can have severe impacts on the ability of student-athletes to balance the demands of athletics and academics successfully. Our task as faculty, coaches, staff, and academic advisors, therefore, is to help provide a conducive atmosphere and a support system that will enable student-athletes to succeed in academics as well as in their sports. The reality that very few of them, if any, especially those from small Division III schools such as Shaw University, will make it to the professional level in their sports must be drummed into them at an early stage in their college career and be reinforced as often as possible throughout their stay in college. The fact is that only 5 percent of high school athletes make college teams, and only 1.7 percent spend at least one year on a professional sports team (Tucker, 1999). Student-athletes have to be motivated and encouraged to work toward acquiring a sound education that will make them competitive in the job market outside professional sports. In this regard, one writer noted: "The overwhelming majority of student-athletes will never earn a dime as a professional athlete. That's why the terms 'student' and 'athlete' are synonymous within the NCAA. When the athlete can no longer play the student can still succeed" www. ncaa.org/wps November 2006.

There is the concern that schools sometimes compromise the integrity of their academic programs in order to foster their athletic programs. In response to this concern, a kind of advocacy group known as The Drake Group (TDG) was established. The mission of the group, as described by Lanter (2006), "is to help faculty and staff defend academic integrity in the face of the burgeoning college sport industry. The Drake Group's national network of college faculty lobbies aggressively for proposals that ensure quality education for college athletes" (p.4). The Group also provides support for faculty whose job security is threatened because of their actions to uphold academic standards. By the same token those institutions and individuals (e.g., athletics officials) who behave in ways that compromise the integrity of their academic programs are subjected to stiff disciplinary actions, including suspension from participating in athletic competitions and/or the loss of very lucrative positions. The recent situations involving the athletics programs at the University of North Carolina at Chapel Hill and Pennsylvania State University are clear examples of the NCAA's commitment to uphold high academic standards for student-athletes and non-athletes alike so that the futures of the student-athletes are not jeopardized. This is particularly important for the vast majority who will not turn professional in their sports.

Focused Goal and Objectives of the Study

This study focused attention on the identification of the problems Shaw University student-athletes face in an effort to provide good quality academic advising that would enable them to excel both in athletics and academics without compromising academic quality and the integrity of the university's academic programs. In pursuit of this goal, the following objectives were addressed: To find out ...

1. the major factors that impacted a student-athlete's academic success.
2. the kind and adequacy of provisions the university made to accommodate student-athletes' absences from class due to their athletic commitments.
3. the assistance offered by the coaching staff to help student-athletes succeed athletically and academically.
4. the attitude of faculty towards student-athletes.
5. the kind of relationship that exists between student-athletes and their academic advisors.
6. the extent of student-athletes' knowledge of NCCAA eligibility rules.
7. to find out what student-athletes like and dislike about being student-athletes.
8. the student-athletes' goals in the next five to six years.

Significance of the Study

Student-athletes are very important to a college or university. A successful college athletic program, for example, attracts students to the institution, which translates to increased enrollment and revenue for the institution. Also, a successful athletic program encourages the alumni and other supporters to provide financial assistance to the institution. An institution with a high student-athlete graduation rate, and more importantly, whose graduates go on to graduate school or find attractive, gainful employment in the public and private sectors, will likely attract many students to seek admission. Any project, therefore, that seeks to find ways to better equip student-athletes to balance their athletic and academic responsibilities effectively is of great significance. This study has valuable potential outcomes for both the student-athletes and the university. These include the following:

a. Identification of student-athletes' concerns and the design of appropriate plans to address such concerns.

b. Improved academic advisement of student-athletes.

c. Sensitization of the university community including faculty, staff, and the administration to the unique circumstances of student-athletes and in this way generate more support to help these students succeed.

d. Improved academic achievement and retention of student-athletes.

e. Realization of the preceding outcomes will, in the long-run, have the cumulative effect of attracting potential students to the university.

Procedure

The study adopted a survey methodology. I designed two sets of instruments (a structured questionnaire for the students and an interview schedule for the coaches) which I used for data collection for the study. The questionnaire sought answers related to the objectives of the study. The coaches' interview schedule delved into some key questions pursued with the students so as to corroborate their answers with those of the students or to identify any discrepancies between them. I conducted a pilot study using a small but representative sample of student-athletes drawn from the different athletic programs. Preliminary results from the pilot study were used to modify and produce the instruments used in the final study. I trained some assistants who helped in data collection and analysis.

A total of 120 questionnaires were distributed to the coaches in the various sports. The coaches administered the questionnaires to their athletes in group settings and the completed questionnaires were either picked up by me or they were returned to me by the very cooperative coaches. In all, 85 questionnaires were returned fully completed, reflecting a return rate of 71 percent. I held a focus group meeting with some of the coaches during which they were interviewed. Other coaches who could not be present for the interview were given the opportunity to express their views by completing the instrument on their own. There were seven coaches representing five different sports.

Participants/Sample

The stratified random sample for the study consisted of 85 student-athletes from five athletic programs, namely football, basketball, track and field, baseball, and tennis. Table 3.1 shows a breakdown of the sample based on two other characteristics - major and classification. The majority of the sample (42.4%) consisted of athletes in football, the biggest sports program, followed by basketball (men and women) representing 21 percent; and track and field, baseball, and tennis, which represented about 12 percent each. The largest group of the students (28.2%) consisted of business and public administration majors, followed by computer science (16.5%), allied health, social science, and education. There were very few majors in science, just a little over 2 percent. The majority of the students were juniors (35.3%) and sophomores (21.2 %).

Table 3.1: Characteristics of the Sample.

CHARACTERISTICS		
Type of Sport	**F (Frequency)**	**%**
Football	36	42.4
Basketball		
Men's	11	12.9
Women's	7	8.2
Track & Field/Cross country	11	12.9
Baseball	10	11.8
Tennis	10	11.8
Total	85	100%

Major		
Business & Public Admin.	24	28.2
Computer Science	14	16.5
Allied Health	8	9.4
Social Science	6	7.1
Education	5	5.9

Mass Communication	3	3.5
Humanities	1	1.2
Science	1	1.2
No response/Undecided	23	27.1
Total	**85**	**100%**
Classification		
Freshmen	7	8.2
Sophomores	18	21.2
Juniors	30	35.3
Seniors	12	14.1
No response	18	21.2
Total	**85**	**100%**

Findings and Discussion

This study resulted in important findings with policy and program development implications to serve student-athletes better. The findings are presented and discussed in this section.

Factors that May Impact a Student-Athlete's Academics

Several factors may affect the time available to student-athletes to devote to their studies, such as doing assignments and preparing for quizzes and exams, and consequently, the quality of their academic performance. Among the factors this study revealed were the following:

1. **Time Spent on Practice**: A question on the questionnaire required the students to mention how often they practiced (mandatory practice) per week during the season of their sports. The footballers practiced five days a week for an average of three hours a day, a total of 15 hours a week. Athletes from the other sports (basketball, track & field, baseball, tennis) practiced three to four days a week for two hours a day, a total of between six to eight hours a week. This is a significant amount of time spent every week on the physically demanding activities that are usually necessary to be

in top shape for competitive sports. Some athletes even have to rush to classes straight from practice. I have had such students in my classes over the years. All this practice can limit the amount of time student-athletes have to devote to their studies. After two to three hours of rigorous practice, it can be very challenging to settle down to do some productive studying.

2. **Time Spent Traveling to Competitions**: Added to the time spent practicing each week is the time absent from classes when they travel to compete in their sports. As to the question inquiring how often they traveled to compete during a semester, the most frequently reported response was between eight to ten times a semester. If they have a good season, and they advanced far into the competitions, as has been the case especially for those athletes in football, basketball, and tennis, they may be away in competitions as many as 12 to 14 times a semester. Analysis of their responses to a question on how many classes they missed during a semester because of their travels to compete showed that, on average, they missed between eight to ten classes a semester. This is quite a lot, and it can have important impacts on the students' success in their classes. The university attaches significant importance to class attendance. According to university attendance policy, for a course that meets three times per week, a student is allowed only three unexcused absences; two absences for a course that meets twice per week, and one absence for one that meets once per week (Shaw University, 2005, p.37). Also, importantly, some instructors award points for attendance and/or class participation. One wonders how such instructors accommodate student-athletes who have to be absent from their class because of the demands of their sports. For example, one student reported as follows: "I had an incident where I was absent from class [for] attending a football game in Maryland. I had a test when I got back without time to study." Such a situation puts student-athletes at a competitive disadvantage compared with their non-athlete classmates.

Provision for Missed Classes

I was interested in finding out what provisions the university makes to help student-athletes catch up on the work they missed during the times they travel to competitions. The results are shown in Table 3.2. The most frequently cited response was that the coaches set up study hall with tutors to assist them with catching up on their academics. This response was cited by about 32 percent of the students.

Table 3.2: Provision for Student-athletes' Absence from Class

Response	f	%
Tutors and study hall set up by the coaches.	27	31.8
University provides written excuses for students to give to their instructors.	25	29.4
Instructors allow make-up work/provision to turn in missed work late.	18	21.2
Just give us the excuse [for absence] and make the work up on your own.	8	9.4
None / Nothing / Don't know / not sure.	4	4.7
Other	3	3.5
N	**85**	**100%**

It was also reported that the university provides written excuses for them to give to their instructors to account for their absences. This represented about 29 percent of the responses. One student, who seemed not very happy with this university's effort remarked: "The school is supposed to give excuses but we get them late. Then even if we do have excuses, the teachers [course instructors] sometimes won't let us make it up anyway." However, 21.2 percent, the third most frequently citied response, reported that their instructors allowed them to make up for work missed or to turn in their work late. There seemed to be differences in opinion regarding the question of instructors' willingness to allow them to make up work they had missed. The following verbatim quotations of the students' responses illustrate this point: One student said: "Instructors allow you to make up work with official excuse." That is, if they produced a university excuse for their absence, they were allowed to make up the missed work. But another student reported the contrary. He said: "My teachers don't let me make up the work most of the time unless it's a test." Another student said: "They [instructors] do not give you make-up work. They ask you to read the syllabus and see what it is we did on the day we missed class." Similarly, another student reported: "Sometimes they [instructors] don't let you makeup missed work unless you are a special athlete, because some teachers act funny." However, he went on to add: "But on the other hand, some teachers will work with you." The fact that there were differences in the students' responses to this question makes it a matter worthy of concern, which should be looked into to ensure that all instructors make provisions for the student-athletes to make up work they missed as a result of engagement in their sports.

Interviews with the coaches in fact corroborate the views of the students who reported that their instructors did not allow make-up work. One of the coaches said that some instructors categorically state in their syllabi that they do not allow any make-up work. It is gratifying to note the efforts the coaches make to help their athletes cope with their academic responsibilities. One student wrote: "My coach usually consults with the team members prior to our departure to [confirm] any athletes who may have a major test or quiz. He usually allows us to take those tests before leaving" [i.e. before traveling to competitions]. One would hope that this is a common practice among all the coaches.

When asked about the adequacy of the university's provisions to help them make up work missed because of away games, about 19 percent of them reported that the provisions were very adequate; a little over half of them (53%) reported that the provisions were either adequate or somewhat adequate. However, 28 percent of them indicated that the provisions were either inadequate or very inadequate. This is quite a sizeable number of students who reported negatively. This is a matter that deserves to be looked into by the coaches and the university administration.

University's Provision for Student-Athletes' Dinner on Practice Days

Since most of the athletes' practice schedules do not allow them to have their dinner during the regular cafeteria operating hours, I was interested in finding out what provisions were made to ensure that the athletes were served dinner regularly. I assumed that poor food and/or irregular eating hours could have a negative impact on the students' well-being, and, consequently, on their academic performance. An item on their questionnaire sought their views on the type of provisions the university makes for their dinner on the days they are out practicing. Box 3.1 below presents an assortment of their responses in this regard.

Box 3.1: Students' Responses Regarding the University's Provision for their Dinner on Practice Days

- Food is sent over to place of practice (Spaulding Gymnasium).
- They fed us sandwich and pizza every day during the week.
- Not good. We have to get the food and bring it back to the locker room. It feels as though the café forgets that we would like to eat a hot meal also.
- We always miss dinner and the food they send is not enough.
- Not well. We just get leftovers when the cafeteria closes. Whatever they find to give us.
- In my case with basketball, McDonalds provides us free food at 9:30 p.m. and that's from Mon- Sat. Now with cross country, if the practice runs late, and if the café is closed, then we have to eat the best way we can [That is, they are on their own.]
- If you miss the café due to a long practice, you are out- of- luck, and, also, if you are an athlete, they should give you a meal plan even if you stay off-campus.
- They don't provide meals for the off-campus student-athlete.
- The cafeteria may extend operation hours for the specific sport so they [the athletes] could have a meal.
- Practice is centered around dinner hour. However, if the cafeteria is closed, our coach goes into his pocket and buys us a meal.

It can be seen that student-athletes were not very happy with the provisions the university makes for their meals when they are at practice. Only 43 percent of them responded that they were either very satisfied or satisfied. Twenty-two percent reported that they were only somewhat satisfied, and a sizeable percent (35%) expressed dissatisfaction (unsatisfied or very unsatisfied) with the University's provision for their meals during practice days. Also, it was surprising to find out that no provision was made for the meals of the student-athletes who lived off-campus. However, interviews with the coaches revealed that athletes who lived off campus did so on their own accord and should, therefore, be responsible for their own meals. These athletes, the coaches explained further, are provided a meal package that covers their breakfast, lunch, and dinner seven days a week. This package costs them only $380 per semester, which they claimed was quite reasonable when compared to what a non-athlete pays.

Assistance/Concern by Coaches

I believe that the coaches can and should play a very significant role in helping their athletes succeed both in their sports and in their academic work. Many athletes look up to their coaches for advice in various aspects of their lives. Therefore, an item on the questionnaire sought the students' opinions regarding how supportive their coaches were in helping them cope with the demands of their academic and athletic programs. An overwhelming majority (84 percent) of the students reported that their coaches were either very supportive or supportive of them. Fourteen percent of them indicated that their coaches were somewhat supportive. Only one student reported that his coaches were not supportive. It is very encouraging that the coaches showed great interest in the students' success, both athletic and academic.

The students were asked further to indicate some of the things their coaches did to encourage them to do well in both athletics and academics. A sample of their responses is shown in Box 3.2 below.

Box 3.2: Things Student-Athletes Reported Their Coaches Did to Encourage Them to Succeed

The following is a sample of the most frequently cited things the students reported that their coaches did to encourage them to do well in both academics and athletics.

- Organization of study hall/tutoring
- Monitoring of class attendance and academic progress/penalty for not going to class
- Visit professors personally to check on students' progress
- Provision of positive reinforcement. "…give 'high fives' and verbal compliments" for good efforts
- "Supports academics 24-7."
- Meet with individual students or in groups to discuss problems and issues that may impact students' progress
- "Often calls to see how classes are going even during the off-season"
- "Always tells us to work together. His saying is 'academics before athletics.'"
- Information about Career Day and résumé preparation workshops.
- "I think he does more than enough."

The responses shown above clearly indicate how genuinely concerned the coaches are about helping their student-athletes to become successful in both their academic and athletic endeavors. It was especially commendable to learn about how much emphasis the coaches placed on academics. One could infer from these responses that the coaches provide the type of "empathetic education" which the university's President religiously advocates at the institution. For example, one student wrote of his coach as follows: "Tells me how hard it was when people weren't able to get an education and tells me that succeeding in both athletics and academics will help you become more disciplined and can help you get a nice job." Another student provided a detailed expression of his views about his coach's concern about his welfare. He wrote:

My coach understands that I am here to play tennis, as I am on a scholarship; but he pushes that aside whenever it comes to my school work. He always tells me to put that first because if my grades are not good, I won't be able to play tennis. He also calls me quite frequently to ensure that I am doing well in my classes and that I am comfortable with the teachers & so on. As far as tennis is concerned, he always wants me to do and be the best that I can. He plans with me to see what area needs strengthening and he doesn't stop until he is satisfied with where I am. One thing he doesn't do is stress us. He pushes us to do well in athletics & academics, but he doesn't overdo it.

Attitude of Faculty Towards Student-Athletes

There is a feeling among students, and some faculty, too, that student-athletes are given special treatment by the coaches and school administration. This perception, I believe, can result in negative treatment of student-athletes by some faculty. Such negative treatment can, in turn, negatively impact the student-athletes' work attitude, and consequently, their academic achievement. A question on the questionnaire sought the student-athletes' perceptions of faculty members', particularly their instructors' attitudes towards them. The results are given in Table 3.3. Only 12.5 percent of the responses indicated that the faculty had high expectations of student-athletes. About 33 percent indicated a somewhat high academic expectation, and

Table 3.3: Attitude of Faculty Towards Student-Athletes

Responses	f	%
They have high academic expectations for us	14	12.5
They have somewhat high academic expectations for us	26	32.5
They have low academic expectations for us (In other words, they feel we are not quality college material)	18	22.5

They feel we are pampered – treated better than non-athletes	11	13.8
They are sympathetic/understanding because of our special circumstance having to cope with the demands of academics and athletics	8	10.0
Other	3	3.8
N	90	100%

N> 85 because the respondents were free to choose more than one response.

another 22.5 percent indicated a low faculty expectation. About 14 percent reported that student-athletes were perceived as being pampered and treated better than non-athletes. Student-athletes are perceived in many different ways, some positive and others negative. Speaking to this issue, Shriberg and Brodzinski (1984) wrote:

> College athletes are simultaneously loved and hated, admired and despised … We see them as saviors of the university for the revenue they create, and as pampered, spoiled brats for the benefits they received. … We hear that large numbers do not graduate, yet research shows their graduation rate to be higher overall than that of non-athletes. … We see them as strong, mature, and confident individuals, yet we often learn that they cannot perform in the classroom. Somewhere in the middle of these images lies the real student-athlete (p. 124).

The impact such contrasting perceptions can have on the student-athlete's ability to combine the demands of athletics and academics successfully can be tremendous. This can be particularly hard on the new students who are also trying to adjust to a new school environment and culture. Only 10 percent of the students indicated that the faculty members/ instructors were sympathetic or understanding of their situation as it relates to the responsibility and associated pressure of coping with athletics and academics.

Relationship with Academic Advisor

Academic advising is a relationship between an academic advisor and an advisee. It can hardly be doubted that a positive relationship enhances the success of academic advising. An item on the questionnaire focused attention on the relationship between the student-athletes and their advisors. Table 3.4 summarizes the students' responses in this regard.

Table 3.4: Student-Athletes' Relationship with Their Academic Advisors

Responses	F	%
He/she is very supportive: friendly, courteous, and approachable, demonstrating a genuine concern for me.	33	29.7
He/she keeps in contact with me via email, phone, and note or in person.	7	6.3
He/she is concerned about my overall welfare – personal and academic.	15	13.5
He/she allows sufficient time to discuss my circumstances.	17	15.3
He/she is only concerned about getting me registered for my classes and nothing more really.	17	15.3
He/she does not have high expectations for me – feels I am not capable academically to do /excel in my studies.	2	1.8
He/she hardly asks me about how I do in my athletics.	8	7.2
He/she has never attended any of my competitions.	8	7.2
Other	4	3.6
N	111	100%

N> 85 because the respondents were free to choose more than one response

Most of the students (almost 30 percent) who responded to this question reported that their advisors were very supportive and genuinely concerned about their success. About 15 percent of them reported that their advisors were concerned about their welfare in general and spent sufficient time with them to discuss their circumstances. However, they cited a concern that their advisors' relationship with them was limited to assisting them with registering for classes. This response represented 15 percent of the cases. Sesay's (2004) study which evaluated academic advising at the university came up with a similar finding about advisors' limited understanding of the comprehensive meaning of academic advising. When the students were asked whether they would like to change their current advisors, 73 percent of them responded that they would not change. However, 27 percent of them reported that they would, and this, I think, should be of some concern to the institution, especially the Academic Advising Center.

Student-Athletes' Knowledge of NCAA Eligibility Rules

The NCAA established rules and regulations governing student-athletes' eligibility to participate in competitive sports, athletes' recruitment, and compliance issues, among other things. Colleges and universities employ a person charged specifically with the responsibility to ensure compliance with the NCAA rules and regulations. I was interested in finding out how knowledgeable the student-athletes were about the NCAA rules and regulations. Analysis of their responses showed that close to 66 percent of them were very knowledgeable about the rules and regulations. Another 33 percent of them reported that they were knowledgeable. The students reported that their coaches kept them fully aware and knowledgeable about the rules and regulations. Such a commitment by the coaching staff and the compliance officer, too, helps to keep the student-athletes focused on their academics in order to keep their scholarship and continue to participate in their sports.

Things Student-Athletes Liked about Being Student-Athletes

When asked about what things in particular they liked about being student-athletes, a fairly wide variety of responses was given. See Table

3.5 for details. The most frequently cited response was that being student-athletes was helping them to develop valuable social skills such as

Table 3.5: What Student-athletes Like About Being Student-athletes

Responses	f	%
It helps me develop valuable social skills such as team work, building relations, being a good loser (accepting defeat with dignity), etc…	42	19.4
It helps me develop valuable leadership skills	32	14.8
It gives me quite a good deal of exposure - in school and in the community	35	11.6
It makes me popular among my peers	23	10.6
In general I get treated very well (sometimes better than non-athletes by members of the University community, including staff, faculty, and administrators	17	7.9
I get to travel and know many places I may not have been able to do if I were not an athlete	35	16.2
I get to attend school free of charge	37	17.1
Other	5	2.3
N	216	100

N> 85 because the respondents were free to choose more than one response

working as a team and being a good loser. This was a significant response reflecting 19.4 percent of the total responses to this question. The value of team work for the success of an organization can hardly be overemphasized. Being a team player is a valuable quality employers look for in an applicant. Also importantly, though the main goal in athletic competitions is to win, the ability to accept with dignity the reality of losing can have invaluable impact on character building. This character trait can be a valued asset when applied in the real world outside athletics later in a student-athlete's life. The next most popular response (17.1%) was that being student-athletes enabled them to attend school free of charge. In fact, as many as 91 percent of the study participants had a scholarship. The next most popular responses were that athletics made it possible for them to travel and know many places they may not have known if they were non-athletes; helped them develop valuable leadership skills; and exposed them considerably in school and the community. These responses reflected 16.2 percent, 14.8 percent, and 11.6 percent of the responses, respectively.

Things Student-Athletes Did Not Like About Being Student-Athletes

In addition to being asked what they liked about being student-athletes, they were also asked about their dislikes. As can be seen in Table 3.6, the most frequently cited response (35.2%) was that student-athletes were stereotyped as not being smart, meaning that they were perceived as being not very capable academically. They also expressed a dislike for the perception that they were not serious about academics. This was their next most popular response, reflecting 27.3 percent of the responses. Such stereotypic and negative perceptions of student-athletes can have a negative impact on their self-esteem whether or not they showed or admitted it. The physical

Table 3.6: Students' Dislikes about Being a Student-Athlete

Responses	f	%
It is very demanding physically and or emotionally.	19	19.2
I don't have enough time to study, and therefore, do not perform to my full potential.	16	16.2
The stereotypic perception of people about athletes is that they are not smart or very capable academically	35	35.2
The perception about athletes is that they are not serious about academics.	27	27.3
Other	2	2.0
N	99	100

N>85 because respondents were free to choose more than one response.

and/ or emotional demands of being student-athletes ranked third (19.2%) among their dislikes about being student-athletes. Related to the demands of their sports was that they did not have enough time to devote to their studies and that this consequently did not allow them to perform to their full potential academically. Sixteen percent of the responses represented this dislike. It can hardly be doubted that the demands of long hours of practice, coupled with taking part in competitions do take away from the student-athletes' time to devote to studying and completing assignments. Absences from class due to travel to competitions exacerbate the problem student-athletes face in trying to balance academics and athletics. However, when asked the question "If you have complete choice, would you prefer not to be a student-athlete, that is, just be a regular student and give up athletics?" the response was a resounding "no," as reported by 87 percent of them. This suggests that the benefits they derived from being student-athletes far outweighed the disadvantages.

Student-Athletes' Plans/Aspirations

Analysis of their responses to the questions relating to their academic and occupational aspirations revealed a very positive outlook. About 91 percent of them reported that they were going to remain at Shaw University until graduation. However, when asked whether they would drop out of school and turn professionals in their sports if the opportunity presented itself, a sizeable percent (38.3 percent) indicated that they would make such a move. Of those who expressed this desire, 74 percent of them were football players. However, close to 60 percent of the sample said they would not drop out to go professional.

The students were asked about their goals for the next five to six years, that is, after they would have completed their undergraduate studies. The majority of them (34.8 percent), as can be seen in Table 3.7, aspired to continue their education at the graduate level. The most popular choices of major were business, law, computer science, criminal justice, and education. This aspiration to pursue graduate studies was common among the students, irrespective of their area of athletics.

Table 3.7: Student-Athletes' Goals (5-6 Years)

Responses	F	%
Pursue graduate studies	31	34.8
Get a good-paying job	18	20.2
Own and operate my own business	15	16.9
Become a coach/work with kids	12	13.5
Play professional sports	8	9.0
Other	5	5.6
N	89	100

N> 85 because the respondents were free to cite more than one response.

Twenty percent of them would like to get a good-paying job, or become self-employed running a business (16.9 percent). They also expressed a desire to become a coach and, in that capacity or a similar one, work with kids. About 14 percent of them expressed this aspiration. Only a few of them (5.6 percent) aspired to become professionals in their sports – that is, play at the professional level. This aspiration was limited to the student-athletes in football and basketball. It is gratifying to note the students' aspiration for careers outside professional sports. Sometimes parental expectations and pressures lead student-athletes to pay disproportionately greater attention to their sports than to academics in order to fulfill their parents' dreams that they would get a professional sports contract. A University of California at Los Angeles (UCLA) study, as cited by Curry (1999) found that "black families are four times more likely than white families to view their children's involvement in athletes as something that may lead to a professional sports career" (p.160). The students in this study, all African Americans, did not appear to be under the influence of such family pressure or they were simply realistic about their aspirations. The fact that very few athletes from small athletic programs such as those of Shaw University ever get recruited to play in the "pros" may account for the low aspirations for this career choice. It is an important reality which the students may have come to accept early in their college life. The great emphasis the coaches placed on academic success, as noted earlier, may also be responsible for the students' realistic career aspirations, particularly with regards to professional sports.

Summary, Suggestions, and Conclusion

Summary

The purpose of this study was to find out the kinds of problems or factors that student-athletes encounter as they try to balance the demands of athletics and academics. The ultimate goal was to find ways in which these students could be more effectively supported to ensure their success in both their athletic and academic endeavors. To provide them with effective academic advising in this regard was a major expected outcome of the study. A total of 85 student-athletes took part in the study. They came from football, basketball (men and women), track and field, baseball, and tennis.

Prominent among the findings were the following:

- A general dissatisfaction with the provision made by the university for their meals during practice days. They complained about the poor quality of the food and the late dinners due to the closure of the cafeteria by the time they got off practice. Commenting on this subject, one student wrote: "The cafeteria doesn't have good food. They feed us like we are elementary children, e.g., grilled cheese sandwiches for dinner." Student-athletes who lived off-campus complained that no food was provided for them after practice.
- Not all professors allowed student-athletes to make up for work they missed as a result of their travels to compete in their sports even though they presented official excuse issued by the university for their absence from class. The coaches interviewed also expressed a serious concern about this problem.
- Some faculty members had negative attitudes toward student-athletes, such as having low academic expectations of them.
- Though most of the students reported a positive relationship between them and their academic advisor, some advisors'

relationship with them was limited to getting them registered for classes. For academic advising to be more effective, it has to go beyond assisting students to choose their courses and register for class. Good academic advising should take cognizance of and address all factors, academic and non-academic, that may impact a student's chances of success. This is particularly relevant for the student-athlete who tries to balance the heavy demands of an athletic program and those of their academic programs.

- Unequal treatment of athletes. Some student-athletes complained that athletes in some sports received preferential treatment compared to their counterparts in other sports. This view was supported by the coaches interviewed.

- The students expressed very strong positive views regarding their coaches' attitudes towards them: The coaches were very supportive, and genuinely interested in seeing them succeed not only in athletics but, more importantly, in academics. The coaches made sure they attended study hall regularly as well as monitored their class attendance and academic progress. They also made them fully knowledgeable of the NCCA eligibility rules which enabled them to maintain their eligibility to participate in athletics.

- Most of the students, irrespective of their sports, aspired to pursue graduate studies, mainly in business, computer science, law, and education. This was very impressive. It somehow dispels the stereotypic perception among some persons including faculty that student-athletes are not academically ambitious.

Suggestions

In the light of the major findings presented in the preceding sections, I offer the following suggestions to help make the task student-athletes face in trying to balance academics and athletes less difficult.

- The coaching staff, the cafeteria staff, and the university administration, with input from the student-athletes, should brainstorm on how best to provide nourishing meals for the student-athletes upon their return from a day's practice.

- In addition to the above, the university administration and the Academic Advising Center should, as a matter of urgency, inform all faculties about the importance for them to provide opportunities for student-athletes to make up work they miss when they travel to participate in competitions. There should be consequences for faculty who do not comply. It is critically important, however, that a more efficient way of documenting such absences be developed to assist faculty in keeping records of class attendance. For example, training of faculty in the use of Jenzaba and Moodle technologies in taking students' attendance should be intensified.

- It is critically important that student-athletes, particularly underclass athletes (freshmen and sophomores) be taught how to manage their time more effectively and efficiently to enable them to combine academics and athletics, as well as take advantage of extracurricular activities to enrich their college experience.

- The university administration should stress the importance for faculty to have higher academic expectations for both athletes and non-athletes in their classes and strive to assist all students to achieve success.

- Faculty advisors should be made fully aware of the fact that academic advising entails more than just assisting student to register for classes. Special populations such as student-athletes require additional support to help them cope with the demands of balancing academics and athletics. This will require the Academic Advising Center to organize training workshops for faculty advisors on a regular basis.

- Because of the tremendous demands posed by a usually hectic academic and athletic college career, academic advisors of student-athletes should ensure that their advisees do not take a heavy course load, especially during the semester when they go out competing in their sports, that is, the on-season. Moreover, they should take only a few of the very demanding courses during this season.

- All student-athletes must be treated equally by their coaches, the university administration, cafeteria staff, and others, irrespective of their sport. Preferential treatment of some athletes (usually because of the popularity of their sports) should be discouraged.

- The University should publicly acknowledge the coaches, all of them, for the great work they do in nurturing their student-athletes, most especially for constantly emphasizing the importance of academics. Their role as mentors, counselors, advisors, and sometimes parents needs to be acknowledged in public forums such as convocations, awards day ceremonies, and in the university publications.

- Greater efforts should be made to help student-athletes prepare to enter graduate school. Most of them have aspirations to pursue graduate studies. A concerted effort by the coaches, academic advisors, the Academic Advising Center, and the Career Development Center should take an active role in this connection.

Conclusion

Research has shown that effective academic advising positively impacts students' satisfaction, retention, and graduation (Gardner, 1995). Also, as Kramer (2003) notes, "other than teaching no other college activity seems to enjoy more legitimacy than academic advising" (p.1). It is crucially important, therefore, that the university gives top priority to providing a sound and comprehensive academic advising program that will benefit its diverse student population. Different categories of students will require somewhat different approaches and emphases in order for the students to benefit fully from academic advisement. Student-athletes constitute one such category of students who require some special services to enhance their college career.

Student-athletes face the challenging task of combining the demands of both their academic and athletic programs. Compounding this task of balancing athletics and academics, the student-athletes have to meet NCAA rules and regulations or lose their scholarship, engage in rigorous practice at least twenty hours a week, miss several classes during a semester due to travel to compete in their sports, and have to deal with some instructors not particularly understanding and accommodating of the pressure-filled circumstances of these students. It is a fact that many student-athletes enter college without as strong an academic background as the general student body, so it is imperative that the institution provide special academic support programs for them. I totally agree with Gerdy, as quoted by Curry (1999), that such support programs "cannot be termed a luxury; rather they are an institutional responsibility" (p. 162). Without a proper supportive program, Gerdy commented further, student-athletes "succumb to the 'just stay eligible' of college life." Recent research, notes Lanter (2006), has indicated "that athletes are not receiving the same cognitive benefits from undergraduate education as other students despite similar academic and personal goals." Lanter cites the works of Pascanella and Truckenmiller (1999) and Ferrante and Etzel (1991) that expose this unfortunate state of affairs in higher education. There is a need for a well thought-out and designed student-athlete support program run by qualified personnel from diverse academic and professional backgrounds. Such an endeavor should receive an unwavering commitment and support from the university administration, the faculty, staff, and the entire university community. A concerted effort of this nature will facilitate the total person approach to the development of a student-athlete program. This approach seeks not just to maintain "an acceptable grade point average or keeping student-athletes eligible for competitions but the social, psychological, and career needs must be met" (Curry, p.162).

It is gratifying to note that the resources and the environment conducive to developing a student-athlete program that adopts the total person approach are available at Shaw University. This study reveals, among other things, a very dedicated and highly committed group of coaches who stress both athletics and academics; a faculty, most of whom are willing to work with student-athletes to ensure their academic success; and a body of student-athletes themselves deeply committed to their sports and academics, and with aspirations to continue their education at the graduate level. The task, then, is to find ways to mobilize these resources efficiently and effectively in ways that will maximize the realization of student-athletes' potentials and ensure their success in college and after college.

References

Bloom, J.L. & Martin, N.A. (2002). Incorporating appreciative inquiry into academic advising. *The Mentor: An Academic Advising Journal.* August 29

Crocket, D. in Wes Habley (2003). Realizing the potential of academic advising. NACADA Summer Institute, St. Charles, Illinois.

Curry, C. (199). From under prepared to academic success: A case for student-athlete support programs and their priorities. In Duhon-Ross, A. Reaching and teaching children who are victims of poverty. Lewiston, N.Y.: The Edwin Mellen Press.

Ender, S. E. &Wilkie, C.J. (2000). Advising students with special needs. In V.N. Gordon, R.H. Wesley & Associates. San Francisco: Jossey-Bass.

Ferrante, A.P. &Etzel, E. (1991). Counseling student athletes: The problem, the need. In E.F. Etzel, A.P. Ferrante, & J.W. Pinckney (Eds.). Counseling college student athletes: Issues and interventions. Morgantown, WV. Fitness Information Technology.

Gardner, J. (1995). In Tom Brown. Advice that matters: What do students hear and remember? Paper presented at the NACADA National Conference, Dallas, Texas. October, 2003.

Kramer, G.L. (Ed.) (2003). Faculty advising examined: Enhancing the potential ofcollege faculty as advisors. Bolton, MA: Anker Publishing Company, Inc.

Lanter, J.R. (2006). Academic advising and college sports: Reclaiming the academic priority. Paper presented at the NACADA 2006 National Conference, Indianapolis, Indiana, October 18-21,

Pascarella, E.T. &Truckenmiller (1999). Cognitive impacts of intercollegiateathletic participation: Some further evidence. *Journal of Higher Education*, 70, 1-26.

Sesay, A.A. (2005). Students' Perspectives on Academic Advising at Shaw University: A Report of Research. Unpublished manuscript.

Shaw University (2005). Undergraduate Catalog 2005-2006. Raleigh, NC: Shaw University, p.37

Shriberg, A. &Brodzinski, F.R. (1984). Rethinking services for college athletes. San Francisco: Jossey-Bass

Walter, T.L. & Smith, D.E.P. (1989). Student athletes: In M.L. Upercraft and J.N. Gardner (Eds.). The freshman year experience. San Francisco: Jossey-Bass.

CHAPTER 4

Talk the Talk and Walk the Walk: An Eye-Opening Experience for Successful Academic Advising

Introduction

The subject of this chapter points to an important personal lesson I learned about honoring the promise we make to others, in this case to our students. When we as teachers or administrators fail to live up to our promises to our students, this may have ripple consequences on their development. For example, when we fail to honor our promises, we are likely to lose their trust, a key ingredient in establishing a congenial work relationship with our students. The lack of trust can have far-reaching consequences on a student's progress. Therefore, when we "talk the talk" (make promises), we must ensure that we "walk the walk" (follow through with our promises).

The impetus for writing this chapter came from a personal experience I had about ten years ago with one of my academic advisees in the Department of Education at Shaw University. For anonymity, I have chosen to a call her Wendy. After a semester's absence from school, Wendy stopped by my office one morning to discuss the possibility of returning to continue her program. "Hi Wendy, how are you and where have you been?" I inquired. She replied that she had been staying alone off-campus and that she had been having problems with her boyfriend. Touched by her story and depressing situation, I "talked the talk" by making her a promise: "From now on, I'll make sure I call you at least once a week to find out how you are doing." Impressed by my words, Wendy thanked me and left after about an hour's visit.

For some reason that I cannot remember as at this time of writing, close to ten years ago, I failed to keep my promise to Wendy. When she returned a semester later to see me to discuss her possible return to continue her studies, I greeted her, but she was unusually cold in her response. I had no problem understanding why. What she said next rang in my head and invoked in me a strong feeling of guilt and sadness whenever I saw her over several years after that meeting. Looking like she was close to tears, she said: "Oh, Dr. Sesay, you promised you were going to call and check on me. Each week I waited for your call but you never called." All I could do was apologize to her and offer no excuse for my failure to honor my promise. I had never felt so saddened and guilty for failing my student.

I am glad Wendy returned to the university, changed her major, and graduated. I thank God also that she never held my negligence against me. We are still friends. After that incident with Wendi, I have been more mindful of what promises I make to my advisees or to any student, for that matter.

From my experience with Wendy, I developed a scholarly conference presentation on the subject of academic advising, which I entitled *"If you Think This Cannot Make a Difference, Think Again: Some Commonsense Tips to Enhance Academic Advising."* The paper, presented at a national conference organized by the National Academic Advising Association (NACADA), was very well received and very positively evaluated by the audience of mostly college and university faculty and administrators. The paper generated a lot of enthusiastic participation from the audience because its contents touched on some real issues and personal experiences having to do with relationships between us, as teachers and administrators, and our students. What follows is a discussion based on findings from a study of academic advising I conducted at Shaw University. Also, I offer some examples of advisement scenarios or problems, some hypothetical but most based on real school experiences to emphasize the importance of establishing and maintaining a healthy relationship with our students such as my Wendy. I provided what I call "commonsense advice/suggestions" to address the various situations contained in the findings from my research study and the academic advisement scenarios.

Premises for the Work

First of all, I present the following premises which guided the discussions alluded to above.

This work was undertaken based on the following premises:

- Academic advising is a lot more than assisting students to select courses for registration. Rather, academic advising is concerned with assisting students to realize the **maximum** educational **benefits** available to them to better **understand themselves** and to learn to use the **resources** of the institution to meet their **special** educational needs (David Crocket).
- Academic advising is a form of teaching.
- Good academic advising is the single most underestimated characteristic of a successful college experience (G. L. Kramer, 2003).
- It takes the whole "academic village" to advise students effectively.
- It takes some commonsense perspectives and actions to enhance academic advising.

Findings from a Study of Academic Advising

The following are quotations from students' responses to questions I raised in the study. Each quotation expresses a complaint about their experience with student advising. Following each complaint is my suggestion for addressing it.

Student Dislikes

- "The only thing I do not like [about my academic advisor] is that sometimes I don't get the same respect that other students get."

Suggestion:

- Be fair and respect every student regardless of age (traditional vs. non-traditional), perceived academic potential, gender, race, ethnicity, socioeconomic status, etc.
- [My advisor is] "bossy and too busy to talk."

Suggestion:

Be professional at all times – approachable, cool-headed, and polite. If you are busy, politely reschedule the meeting with an advisee. Sometimes our office hours include "Other times by appointment". Remember that and honor it.

- "She doesn't know about any of my personal accomplishments outside of the department."

Suggestion:

Take time to know your advisees – academic, as well as non-academic (e.g., acknowledge advisee's accomplishment at work or athletic competitions and recognize the advisee for civic responsibility, performance in the choir/band, etc.). This makes them feel you are interested in their overall well-being and not just in their classroom performance.

- "Not returning calls." I fully understand that the advisors are busy; however, not being able to go to them directly is a problem. So returning calls is important [Response of a CAPE/distant location student]

Suggestion:

Return all calls and in a timely fashion.

Listen to the entire message.

Take notes, research students' questions/problems.

Leave a return message responding to the advisee's question/problem. Don't just say "Mr. Joe, this is Dr. Manner. I'm returning your call" and hang up.

Advisement-Related Scenarios

Scenario I: Stop for even just a minute to smell the roses.

- Professor Busiton is in the elevator with some students. He hits the 4th floor button where his office is located. Lectures are held in classrooms on the first floor only. Professor Busiton stares at the ceiling of the elevator, says nothing to anyone, and dashes out of the elevator when the door opens on the 4th floor. "Did he think we were all going to the 4th floor?" One of the students enquired of the others.

Suggestion:

Don't be so much in a rush and be so self-absorbed that you fail to show some consideration for others, especially our students. Such an attitude by Professor Busiton can negatively impact our relationship with them and may produce poor academic advisement results.

Scenario II: What we say can be hurtful to students

- Dr. Nowell has recently taken up a teaching position in the Chemistry Department of Kaziton College. The chair of his department hands him the folders of his 12 advisees. Three of

Dr. Nowell's students are in his office to sign up for tutorials. Two of his colleagues in the department pop in to invite him to lunch. "Hi guys, why do I get all the dorm students to advise," Dr. Nowell asks his colleagues in a rather angry voice. The students in the room look at each other in dismay.

Suggestion:

Be careful what we say about our students especially in the presence and hearing of other faculty members. We may unintentionally prejudice some colleagues to treat students unfairly and inappropriately.

Scenario III: Student's interest/welfare v. ours

- Lamont is an "A" student in the elementary education at St. Almond College. He is the only person in his family of six to have attended college. His mother is disabled and unemployed and his father works two jobs to support the family. They live in a small two-bedroom apartment. Lamont's advisor left to take up a more lucrative job in industry and you have been asked by the chair of the Elementary Education Department to take over Lamont as your advisee. During your first meeting with him, he says he is thinking of changing his major to one that would enable him to get a better-paying job than teaching. Lamont is one of the few students in the department who has passed the Praxis I test to qualify for formal admission into teacher education. [The department hardly graduates more than 5 students a year].

How can we advise Lamont?

Suggestion:

Be realistic and unselfish. Consider Lamont's family situation and advise him appropriately. The change of major may be a crucial decision the student will have to make. Don't be selfish and advise him to stay in Elementary Education. Yes, a promising student would increase the department's Praxis I pass rate and help put the department in a better position for re-reaccreditation of its programs. But the student's interest and future should come before the department's!

Scenario IV: Every call is important

- You are in your office and the phone rings. You look at the phone and see it's one of your advisees calling. You ignore the call and continue your conversation with a colleague who stops by to gossip about salary discrepancies in your department. "Who was that?" your colleague enquires and you reply, "Oh, one of those advisees with countless problems."

Do you think anything is wrong with respect to this scenario?

Suggestion:

Answer the call! You never can tell the reason for the student's call. She may need your advice to help make a crucial decision that may have a far reaching impact on her education and future. You can tell her to call later or that you will call back. But don't ignore the call!

Scenario V: Our remarks to students have weight.

The following is a true story that illustrates the impact of what we say on our students' future.

Example: Story of Ms. B, North Carolina Teacher of the Year 2006

Ms. B. was busy as usual with her students in her science class.

A student came into the classroom with a message for her. "Ms. B, there is a man in the office who wants to see you," the student said.

One of Ms. B's former students she had taught in 9th grade was returning home from an 18-month deployment in the war in Iraq. He was in his full military attire.

He had stopped by to say hello to Ms. B.

"Send him in," Ms. B told the student who had brought the message.

In came this big, handsome, well dressed and groomed young soldier.

Ms. B. and the young man hugged for a few minutes, looked at each other, and hugged again.

The young man said: "Ms. B, I came to see you before going home. I have just arrived from Iraq where I spent 18 months in the war zone. You once told me that someday I was going to be a great man. I just stopped by to let you know I am now a great man. Thanks for believing in me, Ms. B. Almost the entire class including Ms. B was in tears.

Believe in your students! Inspire them! Be another Ms. B!

CONCLUDING TIPS

- Be sensitive to students' personal problems:

I am not by any means suggesting that academic advisors become psychotherapists and social workers, but I am suggesting that being alert to personal problems that may be getting in the way of students' academic success is an essential part of being an effective advisor for today's students.

- Note that traditional and non-traditional students have different concerns and circumstances and treat them accordingly. See the discussion of this subject in Chapter 5.

- Get to know your advisees. Call them by name and keep their pictures in their folders so that you can always connect their faces to their names.

- Take out an advisee's folder and review it before he/she shows up for an appointment. This gives the student the impression that you are organized, up to your duty as academic advisor, and interested in their welfare.

- Respect diversity and demonstrate it in your words and actions. Remember the adage that action speaks louder than words.

- Don't talk disparagingly about your advisees to other students or your colleagues because they will resent you if you do. Certainly, that will have a negative effect on your advisee- advisor relationship.

- Be approachable – don't go around with a frown. Smile even if it may at times be forced. It's best, though, to be real!

- Stop to say hello to students. A simple hello, smile or wave can make a student's day. The little things we may consider unimportant may be the ones students will value a lot and which may have the most impact on their lives on campus.

- Say some kind/uplifting words to a student, especially one who may be looking sad or depressed. Compliments are a good tonic for uplifting low spirits.

- Attend students' activities – at school and extra-curricular. It may mean quite a bit to a student-athlete, for example, to see you cheering her during a basketball game. Commend her in class about her performance. For example, you may say "That was a great shot, Tamika."

- Be professional and polite on the phone even if you are having a bad day. Never take out your bad mood on an innocent student.

- Keep a neat and organized office. Consider yourself a role model for your students.

- Be truthful! Don't knowingly give wrong information. Research and get some real answers to share with your students.

Note:

- Some of the most important impacts we as advisors make on our students' lives are derived from the little, commonsense things we say to and do with them outside the classroom. Those are the things they remember the most.
- Sometimes it takes only commonsense to advise a student. The little things we may think are unimportant may have far-reaching consequences on a student's future.
- Take your academic advisement role as seriously as you do that of teaching your courses because academic advising is an integral part of teaching.
- Be particularly mindful of promises we make to our students/advisees and to do all we possibly can to keep those promises. Think of the case with Wendy and learn from it!

Remember also that it takes the whole "academic village" to advise a student. The cooperation of the faculty, administration, and staff is essential for successful academic advisement and our students' success.

References

Crocket, D.M. Wes Habley (2003). Realizing the Potential of Academic Advising, NACADA Summer Institute, St. Charles, Illinois.

Kramer, G.L. (Ed.) (2003). Faculty Advising Examined. Enhancing the Potential of College Faculty as Advisors. Bolton, MA: Anker Publishing Company, Inc.

CHAPTER 5

Traditional and Non-Traditional
Students in the College Classroom

Introduction

Advances in medical technology and education are making it possible for people to live longer, productive lives. People stay in the workforce longer than they did in the past. Banks (1999, p.36) noted that the United States population was becoming increasingly older pointing out that in 1980 about 12.5 percent of the nation's population was made up of people over the age of sixty-five and that by the year 2032 this percentage will grow to 22. As the number of this segment of our population increases there will be a corresponding increase in the number of retirees but not in the number of younger workers to contribute toward the retirement of the former. The need for people to continue working long after their retirement age will become inevitable, as is already happening in today's economic times. Also, in order to cope with the demands of the increasingly technological workplace, for instance, many older persons are going back to college to complete their degree, to retool, or to update their knowledge and skills in order to become more competitive and marketable. Some are venturing on a college career for the first time, and others enter college after retirement just for the sake of fulfilling a personal ambition and the desire to broaden their intellectual horizons. What this means is that the population of this category of students, the so-called non-traditional students (25 years of age and older) will continue to increase in our community colleges, four-year colleges and universities, and other higher education institutions. Many of these institutions are opening up new programs or enhancing current ones to recruit and cater to the needs of this population of non-traditional students. On the other hand, as the attainment of a college/university degree is becoming an increasingly significant factor to prepare oneself to compete favorably in today's job market, 18-year old high school graduates, the so-called traditional students, will also continue to grow in our colleges and universities. There is also a small percent of traditional students, about one percent, who enter college under the age of 18. The Southern Regional Education Board's (SREB) *Fact Book on Higher Education* of 2011 notes that "although college enrollment rose from 2005-2009 in nearly every age group nationwide, students 24 years old and younger remained the largest percentage in every region in 2009"(p.36). As a percent of U.S. population enrolled in college in 2009, traditional students 18 to 24 years of age accounted for 38.4 percent. Their non-traditional counterparts ages 25 to 34 accounted for 11.2 percent and those aged from 25 to 49 for another 6.8 percent.

It is important to note that increasing numbers of traditional students, like their older counterparts, also work during the day and take evening and night classes. This means that there will continue to be a fairly good mix of traditional and non-traditional students in college and university campuses across the nation. These two categories of students bring to the classroom a diversity of rich cultural background experiences. It is important, also, to note that our nation is becoming increasingly culturally diverse as more and more people from around the world continue to immigrate for one reason or the other, including political and economic reasons. The point I am making here in regard to this immigration trend is that in some of the countries from which the immigrants come, the factor of age is critically important to their culture. In many African, Asian, and Native American societies, for example, old age is revered; it carries a lot of respect. Older persons, not just those in their 60s and older, but those even in their 30s as well, who are much older than the traditional student, are treated with respect by the younger generation, irrespective of the older persons' educational or social status. Into our classrooms will come non-traditional students from different nations, which will further affect the dynamics of the classroom environment. We live in a multicultural society which is no longer a *melting pot* but a *salad bowl*. The Melting Pot or Amalgamation Theory which requires that all peoples of a society "melt" into a common culture has given way to the more realistic *Salad Bowl Theory*. This theory, in essence, holds that people, while sharing a common macro or mainstream culture, must not abandon or reject their unique micro-cultures in order to be assimilated into the macro-culture. This is a very important point we as instructors should understand as we perform our task of facilitating learning in the classroom. Teaching and learning can be greatly enhanced, and more importantly, made more enjoyable, if instructors can help create a congenial atmosphere to facilitate a sense of belonging, understanding, and mutual respect among the traditional and non-traditional students who will occupy our classrooms.

Adult learners, as non-traditional students are commonly called, come to the college classroom with a wealth of experiential learning. As a result of their personal and professional experiences, Mulqueen (1995) noted, "their level of cognitive development is usually more advanced than the typical eighteen years old" (p.2). The ability to identify the level of reasoning learners have attained will be invaluable in assisting them as they transit back to college. Perry's (1981) study on cognitive development lends credence to the importance of understanding a student's cognitive development as a basis for successful teaching. Several authors (e.g., King and Kitchener, 1994, Zachary, 1985, Daloz, 1986) have supported Perry's findings. It must be remarked also that some non-traditional students, irrespective of their wealth of experiential learning, come to college with comparatively weaker academic backgrounds than their younger traditional student counterparts, especially in the areas of science, mathematics, computer science, and other areas requiring some background knowledge and skills in technology.

Purpose and Objectives of This Study

The purpose of the study on which this chapter is based was to explore ways in which we, as instructors, can effectively create a classroom environment conducive to enabling both traditional and non-traditional students to work cooperatively so that they can derive mutual benefits utilizing the diversity of experiences they bring to our classrooms. The impetus for carrying out the study came from my personal experiences having these two categories of students in my classes every semester over the past several years at Shaw University and observing how they related and interacted with each other, as well as with me. As a multiculturalist and, in fact, the person who introduced the first course in this field at Shaw University, I was always cognizant of the importance of age as an aspect of cultural diversity, even though this aspect has not been given as much attention in research and teaching as the other aspects such as race, ethnicity, gender, socioeconomic status, and language. Also, as an educational policy analyst, I strongly believe that a problem is best addressed when the perspectives of the target population(s) are explored and utilized. With this frame of mind, I decided to survey the views of a sample of traditional and non-traditional students from across the university to find out the following:

- how they felt about being in class with one and other;
- problems they may have relative to the difference in age between them;
- how their instructors interacted with them; and
- the students' suggestions regarding what could be done to help make their college experience as a whole more enriching and worthwhile.

Procedure

Data collection for the survey was carried out with a structured questionnaire which I designed and pre-tested. A total of 300 questionnaires were administered to traditional and non-traditional students selected from across all classifications and majors. A breakdown of the participants is given in Table 5.1. There were 150 traditional students, mostly sophomores, juniors, and seniors, and 92 non-traditional students, mainly juniors, seniors, and others who were not yet classified.

Table 5.1: Composition of the Participants/Sample

Responses	Traditional Students	Non-Traditional Students
Freshman	9	4
Sophomores	42	4
Juniors	51	32
Seniors	48	28
Other (Unclassified)	-	24
N =	150	92

Of the 300 questionnaires administered, 242 were returned fully completed, representing a response rate of 81%. In addition to the questionnaires, a video-taped focus group meeting was held with a sub-group of the participants, during which some key questions raised in the questionnaires were discussed in greater detail. My approach, called by Rossiter (1999) "Narrative Orientation," attempted "to describe development from the inside as it is lived rather than from the outside as it is observed." I was thereby able to generate a breadth and depth of very candid, valuable, and rich qualitative data which I reported verbatim to expand on key issues which the study explored, especially with regards to whether the age gap between the two categories of students had any bearing or impact on their classroom experiences. I believed that using the students' experiences would help me understand them better, and that it would provide me with increased opportunity to create the type of environment that will make our experiences mutually more rewarding and satisfying. The results of the study are discussed in the next section. The results of the analysis of the quantitative data generated by the questionnaires are presented in Tables 5.2-5.4.

Results and Discussion

Analyses of the students' responses are discussed under the following headings:

- Students' feelings about being in class of traditional and non-traditional students.
- Students' assessment of the benefits of taking classes together in a traditional and non-traditional classroom.
- Students' perspectives about their professors' rapport with traditional versus non-traditional students.
- Professors' efforts to provide cooperative learning opportunities for both traditional and non-traditional students.
- Students' suggestions for improving teaching and learning by traditional and non-traditional students.

Students' Feelings about Being in Classes of Traditional and Non-Traditional Students

An item on the questionnaire sought the students' feelings about being in class together as traditional and non-traditional students. An analysis of their responses revealed the results presented in Table 5.2. The majority of the students in each group (48 percent traditional and 32 percent non-traditional) reported that it did not make any difference to them being in class with students of a different age group. However, a sizeable percent of them (27 percent traditional and 20 percent non-traditional) indicated that the factor of age difference motivated them to work harder. The traditional students felt they were more or better prepared for college work than their

Table 5.2: Traditional and Non-traditional Students' Feelings about Taking Classes Together.

	Student	
Responses	Traditional	Non-Traditional
I feel intimidated because I perceive academically than I	9 (5.77%)	8 (4.88%)

I feel confident because I feel I am better prepared.	15 (9.62%)	52 (31.71%)
It makes me work harder.	42 (26.92%)	32 (19.51%)
It makes no difference to me	75 (48.08%)	52 (31.71)
Other	15 (9.2%)	20 (12.20%)
Totals	**156 (100%)**	**164 (100%)**

non-traditional student counterparts. However, only 10 percent of them gave this response compared to 32 percent of the non-traditional students. About the same percent of each group (six percent traditional and five percent non-traditional) reported that they felt intimidated because they perceived the other group as being more prepared academically to pursue college work. Studies have shown, however, that many non-traditional students feel threatened, intimidated, or insecure about returning to college to be in class with much younger students. For example, in her comprehensive and excellent publication, *Guide for Adult College Students*, Goss (1999) recounted many interesting and eye-opening adult students' accounts of their experiences returning to college to take classes with younger traditional students. The following are a few of these accounts:

- It was a terrifying experience for me when I first went back. I went to the state university as a thirty-five year old adult. I was uncomfortable because most of the students were young enough to be my children. But it didn't turn out to be really so bad. I was OK. I found that I did not really care who is what age. I am here to learn and that is all there is to it. Whether they accept me or not socially, I couldn't care. It doesn't matter. I really overcame that fear.

Well, not every adult student may be confident and strong-willed enough to overcome his/her initial fear. For some adult students, one bad experience, especially during the beginning stages of their enrollment, can turn them off and cause them to drop out early or prematurely.

Another student wrote:

- I personally was very threatened about returning, feeling that because I was an older student, there were going to be much younger students in the classroom, much brighter than I, who would probably ridicule me. People can tell you that it will be o.k., but you have to feel it and see it and live with it. Then you find out it is o.k.

The situation can be more uncomfortable and threatening when there are only a handful of these students in the midst of an overwhelming number of traditional students.

Another student wrote:

- Even if you are good in a particular subject, when you go back you are competing against younger kids and younger adults. They're faster. Their way of thinking is faster. My way of thinking was slower. I couldn't keep up with the assignments. It was boom, boom, boom – too fast. I didn't have the time to handle the workload. They [traditional students] can do itin half the time that I canand they probably don't have the distractions that I have, either. I had to cut down on the number of courses I was taking.

Instructors who do not take cognizance of the reality of the non-traditional students' situation and characteristics described in the above quotation can make the college experience for the non-traditional student very threatening and hostile. Assistance, for example, to facilitate a building of good social relationships among the students, can be a productive strategy to promote effective teaching and learning experiences both within and outside the classroom. For example, another non-traditional student was quoted as expressing her views about the relationship between students of her age group and those of her traditional age counterparts as follows:

- The younger students sat by themselves. They looked at us differently. There was no socializing as far as going out for coffee or down to the cafeteria. They stuck by their own and we stuck by our own. I guess that's just natural.

Though it is true that such a situation can be "just natural," as this student put it, it is a responsibility of the instructor(s) to help create the milieu in which to facilitate a healthy living and learning relationship among these two different generations of students. The outcome can be mutually rewarding and satisfying to both groups. We want to create a situation in which a non-traditional student, for example, would feel confident to say in the words of one such students.

- I get along great with the kids. That is not a problem whatsoever. An adult learner can add a lot to a course. The things that we take for granted, the kids are still fumbling over. We can help them. I bring a lot more to some of the courses than the kids do.

A testimonial of this nature, contained in the quotation above, can only be a product of the work of a skilful facilitator of learning.

When I pursued further the question of students' perspective on taking classes together, I found that if they had complete freedom of choice, the results indicated that each group would prefer a mixed class, with a greater percent of the traditional students, 91 percent of them compared to 67 percent of their non-traditional counterparts, reflecting this preference. However, as many as one-third of the non-traditional students expressed a preference to have classes with only members of their age group, assuming they had complete freedom of choice in the matter. The reason for their preference, I am inclined to think, may be because as older students they have more similar backgrounds, including educational, work, and life experiences they bring to the classroom than their traditional students counterparts. Only 9 percent of the traditional students indicated that they would prefer taking classes with only members of their age group, if they had complete freedom of choice. This was a bit surprising to me because I had assumed that because they were much closer in age to each other, and hence, share similar educational backgrounds and socio-cultural interests, the traditional students, like some of their non-traditional counterparts, would have preferred taking classes with only members of their age group.

Students' Assessment of the Benefits of Taking Classes Together

As noted in the preceding paragraph, the majority of both the traditional (91 percent) and non-traditional (67 percent) reported that it was beneficial for them to be taking classes together as traditional and non-traditional students. An item on the questionnaire sought their perspectives on what the benefits were in this regard.

It was interesting and also encouraging to find out that their views regarding the benefits of taking classes together were complementary. They mirrored those of similar students reported in Goss's Guide cited earlier in this chapter. An assortment of verbatim quotations of their views in this regard is presented in Boxes 5.1A and 5.1B, the latter in the record representing the traditional students' views and the former the non-traditional students'.

- Benefits related to improving learning – reflected in the first **10** bullets in italics, and
- Benefits related to preparation for the future/world of work - reflected in the remaining eight bullets.

Box 5.1A: Verbatim Quotations of Traditional Students' Views Regarding Being in Class with Non-traditional Students

---

- *They have been in this world longer and they share more knowledge with us traditional students.*
- *I have gained knowledge on personal experiences of the real world and know how to cope with society. The personal experience and words of wisdom will help me to be a well-rounded teacher.*
- *Well, they can provide me with more information on how to do things such as lesson plans, classroom management, etc. and provide me with the necessary information that they have since they are already within the school system.*

- *Having classes with non-traditional students for the second year has given me more confidence as a future classroom teacher. They have provided me with resources that will help me when I become a teacher, and they give me feedback on what to do to improve my lesson plans or my teaching style.*
- *I can benefit from non-traditional students by the information they give; not that they are more advanced than me, but they are more experienced than me.*
- *It is a good learning experience. You get a better understanding of how older people think. However, they try to dominate the class discussions.*
- *From their experiences you can learn how to cope with pressures of life, and how to stay in balance. That also brings spice and interest to the class based on their experience. I think having non-traditional students in the class sometimes challenges the professor to work, research, and teach even more to make sure they cover the entire subject.*
- *Diversity is what makes the world go round. They [non-traditional students] bring experience and sort of a different level of thinking.*
- *They interacted more in class. They give positive feedback on subjects. Sometimes the experiences they have encountered give us hope.*
- *It is very interesting to know the cultures of other people even here at Shaw. I have learned to study with people other than traditional students. It is a good experience. Some of those students [non-traditional] have become my closest friends.*

- It helps you because when you join the workforce you will already know what you are going to deal with. You even learn the language of the workforce from them [non-traditional].
- They are able to tell you about the pros and cons of different professors and their classes.
- I think a lot of students have benefited from taking classes with non-traditional students because they are older and wiser. I think a person's attitude can change for the better because of a non-traditional student.

- I have benefited from taking classes with non-traditional students. They give us insight into "the real world." They provide us with an example that perseverance in achieving goals is what is important. They have not given up on their educational goals.
- Non-traditional students really have lived and come back for a reason, which makes you see the reason why you should stay in school.
- The older students give inspiration and encourage the young students; they show that if one truly wants an education, all obstacles can be conquered. I have seen many people overcome tough circumstances and become top students. They show me I can do anything if I try.
- Sometimes things I don't understand they can help me [with] when the professor cannot get through to me.
- In my Foundations of Education class I was able to hear actual experiences from a parent and an educator. It made the discussions more meaningful because of the mix of firsthand accounts and philosophical/theoretical discussions.

The non-traditional students' views are shown in Box 5.1B below. As noted earlier, their views for the most part complemented those of their traditional student counterparts.

- Motivation/Inspiration (see the first **six** bullets in italics), and
- Diversity and its positive impacts (see remaining nine bullets).

Box 5.1B: Verbatim Quotations of Non-traditional Students' View on the Benefit of Taking Classes Together with Traditional Students.

- *I like the innovativeness and realness of younger students. Being in class with younger students has made me more aware of issues that I normally would not have considered.*
- *You can always learn something from someone else and you can never know what they can offer. I always keep an open mind for new things.*

- *I can learn from them and they can learn from me. We have much in common as fellow students.*
- *We both have much to offer each other, similar to the views of male vs. female or husband vs. wife. The young students give me more drive and determination and a good outlook on the Afro-America future. The older generation, on the other hand, offers "been there... did that" experience and is a great support system for the youths. I e-mail my classmate Joseph [a traditional student] and call others just to say "hang in there." I like to know how he perceives situations that I can compare to my own "think tank."*
- *Working with traditional students encourages me to work harder, because I feel I should be an example, a role model, etc. I have found the students to be very respectful. I also feel traditional students also are encouraged to work harder realizing that they are on the road to being successful earlier in life, and they are fortunate in this respect.*
- *They give me the incentive to strive to my highest potential. I benefited from taking classes with traditional students because I was able to use their fresh minds to aid me in areas (e.g., math) I might have forgotten since graduating from high school almost twenty years ago.*

- It helps me understand the younger students and their ideas. It also helps with increasing my knowledge base. One is more likely to stay open-minded.
- I have benefited from taking classes with traditional students. Firstly, they keep me thinking young and not becoming an "old foggy." Secondly, I learned how to be a student again after many years.
- Everyone has different life experience that we can learn from. It is always beneficial to hear a perspective from different people (e.g. age, race, gender, etc.).
- From observing them I have gotten a better handle on what university instructors expect from their students.
- Being in class with only non-traditional students takes the flavor out of learning. Both groups compliment the other. It is always necessary to have a fresh perspective.

- I enjoy the composition of my classes. It gives me the chance to not only learn, but also cooperatively learn. It's a lot more fun than having one category of students per class.
- I have learned from them (the young students) and I hope that they have learned from my experience that I have shared. I have enjoyed my "back to school" experience and have learned a lot.
- Listening to the students, I feel thankful having the opportunity to have experienced life as I have.
- We share information with each other as far as assignments are concerned. Also, it teaches me how to interact more with my pre-teenage and young adult children.

Students' Perceptions of How Their Professors Related to Them

I was interested in finding out how professors, most of whom were closer in age to the age group of non-traditional students, related to both categories of students. Is it possible, for example, that the professors, as perceived by their students, treated one category of students better than the other? The results of the analysis of their responses to the item on the questionnaire relating to this issue are presented in Table 5.3.

Table 5.3: Students' Perceptions of How Their Professors Related to Them

	Student			
Responses	Traditional		Non-Traditional	
	F	%	F	%
They professors have a much friendlier and closer relationship with my counterparts.	12	16.82	4	4.30

The professors treat them better. For example, they show more understanding towards them (e.g., turning in assignment late, making up a missed quiz or exam, etc.)	24	13.64	4	4.30
I feel the professors are not as strict in grading their work as they are with ours.	18	10.23	12	12.90
The professors treat us pretty much the same	117	66.48	68	73.12
Other	5	2.84	5	5.38
Totals	**176**	**100%**	**93**	**100%**

As can be seen from the table, the majority of the students in each group reported that their professors treated them "pretty much the same," that is, irrespective of whether they were traditional or non-traditional students. It is a very important finding that the professors in general exhibited a non-preferential treatment to both groups of students. However, there were a few cases in which the students reported some preferential treatment, and that should be a cause for concern to faculty and the university administration. For example, about 14 percent of the traditional students reported that their professors treated their non-traditional student counterparts better – for example, allowing them to turn in their assignment late and making up a missed quiz or exam. If not handled skillfully and professionally, such preferential treatment can be a source of discipline problem for the professor. Also, about ten percent of the traditional students and about 13 percent of the non-traditional students reported that their professors were not evenhanded in grading their work. That is, the professors were not as strict in grading of their counterparts' work. Only one percent of the students reported any major form of "unfair treatment by their professors." I think that a 98-99 percent grade on the report card on "fair treatment by the professors" is cause for celebration, especially since rare abuses will likely be reported.

Allyson A. Sesay, Ph.D.

Students' Views on Their Professors' Provision of Cooperative Learning Opportunities

Cooperative learning is one important strategy a teacher can use to facilitate effective learning in the classroom, because, for one thing, it provides ample opportunities to instructors to facilitate effective interaction among students in the lesson. Students' responses to the question of whether or not their professors provided opportunities for cooperative learning are presented in Table 5.4. The majority of the students (40 percent traditional and 62 percent non-traditional)

Table 5.4: Students' Responses Regarding their Professors' Provision of Collaborative Learning Opportunities.

	Student			
Responses	Traditional		Non-Traditional	
	F	%	F	%
Most times they do	51	39.53	52	61.90
Sometimes they do	48	37.21	24	28.57
They seldom do	21	16.8	8	9.52
Other	9	6.98	-	-
Totals	**129**	**100%**	**84**	**100%**

reported that most times their professors provide such opportunities. Thirty-seven percent of the traditional students reported that such opportunities were provided "sometimes" compared to 29 percent of their non-traditional counterparts. Only a small percent of each group, 16 percent traditional and 10 percent non-traditional, reported that cooperative learning opportunities were seldom provided. Taken together, over 70 percent of both groups reported that professors provided cooperative learning opportunities either "most of the time" or "sometimes." This may be a reason why both groups supported the idea of taking classes together, because this provided important benefits to them, as reported earlier in this section. Having cooperative learning groups, for example, not only enhances students' academic performance but promotes the development of valuable social knowledge and skills, an invaluable student learning outcome.

Students' Suggestions for Improving Teaching and Learning of Traditional and Non-Traditional Students

Though they expressed a few concerns about taking classes together, both groups of students in general supported this teaching and learning arrangement because it enhances their learning. An open-ended item on the questionnaire sought their suggestions for improving teaching and learning when in a mixed class environment. The following verbatim quotations reflected the majority of their views in this regard:

- Have more situations in which cooperative learning or group learning is used.
- Develop more group projects and meet on a regular basis, not just once a week.
- Ask questions about each other. Be eager to learn about someone else's culture and experiences other than you own.
- The professors should have them interact more; group together more.
- Include everyone in the discussion

Recommendations

This study revealed important findings with policy implications for enhancing teaching and learning involving traditional and non-traditional students, two categories of students whose population will continue to grow in our colleges and universities across the nation. I make the following recommendations based on the study's findings:

Professors should do the following:

- Capitalize on the very positive feeling among traditional and non-traditional students about taking classes together and their personal benefits of such a learning environment. For example:

○ Provide more cooperative learning opportunities for both groups to share ideas, experiences, and survival skills. This, in fact, complements the students' own suggestion to enhance their learning.

○ Encourage peer tutoring.

- Provide equitable treatment to all students irrespective of whether they are traditional or non-traditional, especially when it comes to sensitive matters as assessing and accepting students' assignments.

- The university, through the office of Faculty Development, perhaps, should provide on a regular basis effective orientation of faculty on teaching of traditional and non-traditional students. The psychology of learning of adult (non-traditional) students should be an important topic for such an orientation.

- Orientation for both traditional and non-traditional students should be provided, and the subject of these groups taking classes together should be covered. This important subject is not usually addressed during the orientation provided at the CAPE and Raleigh campuses at the beginning of each semester.

- Non-traditional students should be introduced to organizations that advocate for their wellbeing and success.

Conclusion

It was interesting and also encouraging to find out that the views of the traditional and non-traditional students regarding the benefits of taking classes together were complementary. Both groups expressed a strong desire to work together, believing that the experience was mutually beneficial. The task for us as teachers is to ensure that we adopt pedagogical strategies (e.g., cooperative learning) that will facilitate effective teaching and learning for both traditional and non-traditional students. Orientation of faculty members to adult learning is critical for success in this regard. Though traditional students continue to be the greater percentage of college student enrollment in the nation, the percentage of non-traditional students continues to increase. Both these groups of students, especially incoming freshmen, are faced with a variety of exciting opportunities as well as challenges, which may be overwhelming. They, therefore, as I noted earlier, need an effective support system. Without such a system in place to help the students make the necessary socio-cultural, emotional, and academic adjustments to their new environments, the probability for them to not succeed and drop out would be high.

The situation is particularly critical for the non-traditional students entering college at a much older age than the traditional students, the former having to combine the responsibilities of school work with those associated with holding a full-time job or a combination of a full-time and part-time job(s) and taking care of their families. They, therefore, need support not only from within their institutions but also from outside advocacy organizations. One important such organization is the Association for Non-Traditional Students in Higher Education (ANTSHE), "an international partnership of students whose mission is to encourage and coordinate support, education, and advocacy for the adult learning community" (p.1). In realization of the difficulties nontraditional students face in their effort to acquire a college education, former Senator of New York, Hillary R. Clinton, as reported by Kristan Lane (2005) made the following emotional plea on their behalf – "You know these students. You work with them every day. You know they are working hard to finish school, to provide for their families, to do the right thing. And they deserve our support" (Lane, p.1). The Senator, who was at the time the nation's Secretary of State, was proposing the Non-Traditional Student Success Act, which was co-sponsored by her Democratic colleague, Senator Bob Graham of Florida, in an effort to help alleviate the problems these students face in their attempts to further their education. Action by President Obama to increase the Pell Grant award also helps to ease the financial burdens on these students, as well as on their traditional student counterparts.

It takes special pedagogical skills to be able to provide the congenial environment to facilitate effective and efficient learning among traditional and non-traditional students in the same classroom. Ongoing faculty development in this regard is a desideratum for effective teaching of both these categories of students.

References

Blumenfeld, P.C., Kempler, T.M., & Krajcik J.S. (2006). Motivation and cognitive engagement in learning environments. In R.K. Sawyer (Ed.). *Cambridge ... in learning sciences.* New York: Cambridge University Press.

Goss, D. (1999). Guide for Adult College Students. Unpublished Monograph. Curry College.

Johnson, J.A., Dupuis, V.L., Musial, D., Hall, G.E., and Gollnick, D.M. (2002). Foundations of American Education (12th.Edition). Boston: Allyn and Bacon.

Lane, K. (2005). Senator Clinton unveils plans to help non-traditional students. (Dateline Washington): Community College Week, July31, 2005

Santrock, J.W. 2008). Educational Psychology (3rd Ed.). New York: McGraw-Hill.

Slavin, R.E. (1990). Achievement effects of ability grouping in secondary schools: A best-evidence synthesis. *Review of Educational Research,* 60, 471-500.

CHAPTER 6

White Students as a Minority Group in a Predominantly Black University: A Case for Realizing Cultural Diversity and Pluralism

Introduction

An emerging trend in student demographics is the increasing enrollment of white students in predominantly black colleges and universities, where they seek a good quality education at a price much lower than in comparable white schools. Consequently, more and more white students are enrolling at historically black colleges and universities (Drummond, 2000). The social dynamics this situation presents can have significant implications for effective academic advising and consequently, for students' success. While much has been written about the experiences of minority students as they navigate predominantly white campuses, (Banks, 1988, 1994, Upcraft& Stephens, 2000; Burton, 2003; Brown, 2004), relatively little has been written about the reverse situation. How, for example, do white students, especially incoming first year students, cope with being a conspicuous minority group in a predominantly black school? Does the

93

increase in cultural diversity translate into enhanced cultural pluralism on the campus? These are some of the salient questions that have occupied my mind as I see the few white students in my classes or as they walk quietly across the campus here at Shaw University. My purpose for undertaking this study was to explore the experiences of these students as they function in a significantly different cultural environment and to find out how best they could be assisted to cope and succeed.

The impetus for taking on this study comes primarily from personal experiences living and working as a minority in an almost 100 percent white environment to which I was exposed for the first time in my life. Born, raised and educated up to college level in West Africa, I came to Langston University in Oklahoma, a predominantly black institution, to further my education. Though there were some cultural differences, I never felt like a racial minority. Unless I spoke no one could tell I was from a foreign nation. I returned to Africa and worked for eight years at a university in Nigeria and felt quite at home because I blended in easily as an African in an African country. Even as a graduate student at the predominantly white University of Illinois at Urbana-Champaign, a predominantly white institution, where I did my graduate studies, I did not feel myself a minority student because of the presence of a large international student body, including Africans and African Americans.

But the cultural, racial identity and comfort I experienced and enjoyed for many years in predominantly black environments was about to change when I accepted a position as visiting minority faculty at a university in Maine, a state almost 98 percent white. With the exception of one African student, I was the only black person not only at the university but in the whole city where the school was located. Everywhere I went, the bank, the grocery store, a pub (when I was bold enough to enter one), I could feel the "vibes" as people starred at me. Occasionally some folks would hesitate when I stretched out my hand to greet them because it was their first time standing that close to a black person. Once, when I was invited to attend a statewide conference at a popular holiday resort, I felt excited to think I was at least going to meet some folks of my racial background. I was mistaken. Of the over three hundred participants from all the constituent universities of the state system, the public schools, and other education establishments, I was the only person of color. Even as an adult over 40,I felt uncomfortably conspicuous.

Another disturbing personal experience I had as a faculty member in Maine was an encounter with a work-study student in the university library. I was reading some articles in a journal and it was getting to closing time for the day. I decided to check out the journal for overnight use so that I could complete my work, but the work-study student at the checkout desk denied me the privilege for overnight checking accorded to faculty. "We do not check out journals overnight to students," she told me in a rather arrogant tone of voice. Calmly, I replied that I was a faculty member and not a student. To my surprise, dismay, embarrassment, and anger, she turned around to the other students at the checkout desk and inquired, "Is that true?" She wanted to confirm whether, as it was, I was trying to impersonate a faculty member. I was properly dressed, but that did not matter. One of the students came to my rescue and told the enquiring student "He is a faculty. He is my professor." I had "lost my cool" at this point and asked the student "If I were a white man would you have doubted me when I told you I was faculty?" Then she replied with another insulting statement, "You are just being very sensitive." Rather than lose my temper altogether, I simply left and reported the incident to one of the permanent library staff on duty. But I have always wondered whether I would have been treated that way if I were a white man in a predominantly black university. Is there anything like "black privilege" in America, a corollary to what McIntosh (1993) addressed in her famous "white privilege" article? This unanswered question in my mind further aroused my curiosity to explore the phenomenon of whites in a predominantly black environment.

As the only black faculty member and assigned to teach a course in multicultural education, it was not easy discussing topics bordering on race and racial discrimination without making many of my students uncomfortable. For most of them I was the first black instructor they had ever had. I was there during the famous O. J. Simpson trial and questions were raised about my perspective on the racially polarizing trial. I used the Million Man March, which also took place while I was there in Maine, as a subject to discuss the problems of racial discrimination and intolerance, and educational and economic disparities in American society. I could clearly see and feel the discomfort in many of my students as we discussed these and similar issues. I survived in Maine for three years as the only minority faculty member at two of the universities where I worked. All in all, it was a wonderful experience for me, my students, and members of the university community as I shared my cultural background experiences with them.

When I arrived at Shaw University after my three adventurous years of cultural experiences in Maine, I found a handful of white students whom I felt were in a situation similar to mine when I was in Maine. I took special interest in observing how they, especially the young traditional students, got along in class and on campus in a culturally different environment. Since it is the university's mission to provide "educational opportunities for all segments of our society without regard to race, creed, or ethnic origin" (Shaw University, 2010), it is of paramount importance that all students are provided an environment where they would feel, first of all, welcome and wanted; safe, respected, and unafraid to freely express their various points of view. The university's creed "pro Christo et humanitate" (for Christ and humanity) makes this all the more important to provide such an accommodating environment for all students. Rather than simply assume that such an environment exists, it is important to explore the students' perspectives so that we can plan more effectively to meet their needs. This belief fueled my interest and enthusiasm, especially as a multiculturalist, to undertake this study. I am not implying by any means that white students at Shaw University were being treated unfairly, but I just felt it of interest to find out how the majority students feel and cope in an environment where they are in the minority. Although no situation, especially involving human interactions and co-existence, is perfect, I believe that improvement can always take place.

Procedure

Study Participants

I tried to capture the entire population of the only 46 non-African American students enrolled at the university at the time of data collection in the fall of 2004, but I was able to reach only 33 (72 percent) of them. African Americans accounted for 1460 (91 percent) of the total undergraduate student population. These enrollment statistics were, however, not very different from those recorded in the 2010/2011 academic year in which white numbered only 46 (1.8 percent) of the population and blacks 2161 (85 percent). In fact, the white (non-Hispanic) student population remained the same as it was in 2004/2005. There was only a very small percentage change in the white student population between 2004/2005 and 2010/2011, an increase from 1.70 to 1.80 percent (OSPIRE, 2011, p. 51). Table 6.1 shows a detailed breakdown of the participants' characteristics. There were more females than males, 70 percent and 30 percent, respectively. Traditional students represented 38 percent and non-traditional 62 percent. The majority of the participants lived off campus and about 14 percent lived on campus.

Table 6.1: Characteristics of the Participants

Characteristics	F	%
Sex:		
Male	11	29.7
Female	26	70.3
Category:		
Traditional	14	37.8
Non-traditional	23	62.2
Residence:		
On-campus	5	13.5
Off-campus	32	86.5

Research Instruments

I designed and pre-tested two sets of instruments for data collection, a structured questionnaire for all the participants and an interview schedule for a follow-up interview with a sub-set of the participants. A total of 46 questionnaires were administered in person on the Raleigh Campus and with the help of the CAPE Directors at the CAPE locations across the state. A total of 37 (80 percent) of the questionnaires were returned fully completed. Ten students were selected for a follow-up interview based on their particular and insightful responses to the questionnaire.

Luckily, none of the participants was enrolled in any of my courses during the time of data collection which may have allayed any fear of possible victimization by me for expressing views that they may have considered contrary to mine or uncomfortable to me. The interviews were conducted independently in order to ensure that each participant's perspectives were not influenced by another.

Data Analysis

The quantitative data generated from the responses to the pre-coded questions in the questionnaire were decoded and the results presented in tabular form showing frequency and percentage responses. Responses to the open-ended questions in the questionnaire and those in the interview schedule were sorted to discover possible themes. In addition, direct quotations from the participants' responses were cited in the report to enhance/or explicate some key issues raised in relation to the study's objectives and research questions. The findings are presented in the next section.

Findings and Discussion

Choice of Shaw University

I was interested in finding out why of all the many colleges and universities in the state of North Carolina the participants chose Shaw University, a HBCU. Their responses are given in Table 6.2. The most popular response was that they chose Shaw University because of the influence of a team of recruiters from the institution. As a predominantly black (91 percent) institution, it is understandable why the Admission Office would make desperate efforts to recruit more white students in order to increase the ethnic/racial representation in the student population. This was confirmed to be the case by recruiting officials of the university. The federal government is emphasizing the importance of colleges and universities improving their ethnic and racial diversity in both faculty and students.

Table 6.2: Students' Reasons for Choice of Shaw University

Responses	f	%
Influence of a recruiting team from Shaw University	23	42.6
I liked their CAPE Program	13	24.1
A friend/relative encouraged me	9	16.7
The prospect of getting financial aid	4	7.4
Other	2	3.7
No response	3	5.5
TOTALS	**54**	**100%**

N>37 because the respondents were free to mention more than one response

The CAPE program also attracted the students to the university, as was reported by 24 percent of them – the next most popular response. The third most popular reason given for their choice was that a relative or friend encouraged them to apply. For example, one student explained as follows:

- It [Shaw University] was recommended by a friend, a teacher, when I said I was thinking about going back to get my four-year degree to teach. She said, "I've got the perfect place for you. They'll make you feel like you're at home and treat you really nice. She even drove me to the Rocky Mount CAPE. She even drove me there in her car; that's how strongly she felt about me attending Shaw. She's an African American.

As a minority group in a Black institution, seven percent of them said they were motivated to choose Shaw by the prospect of getting financial aid. About four percent of them gave other responses, such as the following statement "The way God led me."

Feelings about being a White (Minority) Student at Shaw University

As I mentioned earlier in this chapter, some of my own experiences as a minority faculty at a predominantly White university sparked my interest in finding out how white folks felt being in the minority. An item on the questionnaire sought the students' views about how they felt being a minority in an overwhelming Black environment on the Shaw University campus. The results showed that 38 percent of them reported that they sometimes felt uncomfortable being in such a minority environment, especially when topics bordering on race or racial discrimination were being discussed in class. The following are samples of verbatim responses of their views with regard to the issue of their comfort in participating in such discussions.

- I think I feel comfortable sometimes; it depends on how the other person is approaching the subject. If they're being very offensive with their speech, then I tend to be uncomfortable, but I still l participate. I don't let myself be pushed aside at all, and I probably tend to be politically correct. A lot of it is rearing, how you were brought up; if you were brought up in a prejudiced family, I would assume that you would take on more offensive life.
- Sometimes when I feel uncomfortable I still participate in the discussion... when I participate, I tend to be politically correct in order not to offend anyone. I always try to be politically correct, whether I'm here or not.
- The only time I can say I feel uncomfortable is when certain topics come up and people get very heated, like they're angry. I'm

not going to say anything, because I'm not going to fight with somebody.

Interestingly, the majority of the students reported that they did not experience any discomfort being in such a predominantly Black environment.

Thirty-nine percent of them reported that the situation made no difference to them and another 21 percent of them indicated that, in fact, they liked the atmosphere (i.e. of being in the minority). The following verbatim quotations reflect the general views of students in this regard.

- I feel alright because they [African Americans] are not only learning about me, I'm learning about them. And I've been accepted by all the students here. I've never had one to not accept me; we're all like family.
- Actually, I'm treated very nicely by the students, professors, the staff, everyone around me; honestly, it may be my attitude. I think that if I came in with a different attitude like I was entitled or like you should treat me better or you should treat me some way, I might not have been treated as nicely. I'm just friendly and open. I think that I'm getting a cultural education as well as an academic education. The schools that I work in, in Greensboro, are predominantly black. And the students I will be working with, I need to know their culture and this is the best way to get it – to be immersed in the culture, to hear how African American people feel about raising their children, about discipline, about these kinds of things, you only get if you're immersed in the culture; if you are in the middle of it, where they'll be honest and open.
- I honestly don't notice that often that I am the minority. I enjoy being able to learn not only in a different culture but also about the culture.
- It didn't bother me because I moved here from New Orleans, a city where whites are the minority. I didn't even know what a HBCU was.

Interesting/Motivating Things about Shaw University

A follow-up question to that on comfortability being in a minority situation sought the students' views regarding what they found interesting or motivating being at Shaw University. Analysis of their responses provided the themes shown in Table 6.3. The most interesting or motivating aspect of the university, as cited by 41 percent of the students, was the friendly and diverse faculty. For example, in expressing her views in this regard, one student wrote as follows:

Table 6.3: Interesting/motivating things students reported about Shaw University

Responses	F	%
The curriculum (e.g. International Studies, Ethics, Cultural Diversity	33	30
Friendly and diverse faculty	45	41
Meeting/making new friends outside my culture	28	25
Other	4	4
TOTALS	**110**	**100%**

N>37 because respondents were free to give more than one response

- ...This faculty is so diverse – what they've done, their experiences in life; some of them have been CAPE students who have come through like I'm coming through, and they have the experience and knowledge of not only the subject matter but of the experiences of life I'm living right now. They can say "you can make it", you can do this, I did it 5 years ago, 7 years ago, etc.

Next in importance of the interesting/motivating things about being at Shaw University the students cited was the curriculum. Thirty-eight percent of them reported this response, and cited the courses in Ethics, International Studies, and Cultural Diversity to be of particular interest. One of them expressed her feelings thus:

- The subjects I'm taking are interesting. I'm learning about different people, different countries, their politics and religions. Your courses in International Studies, Ethics and Diversity are very helpful and informative.

They also reported that "the opportunity of meeting and making new friends outside their culture" was likewise interesting and motivating to them. This response reflected 25 percent of the total responses. Only four percent of them mentioned other things of interest.

On the other hand, the students were asked to mention the aspects or things about the university they did not find particularly interesting or motivating. The analyses of their responses have been categorized under the following two categories or codes:

- Dissatisfaction with university operations
- Dissatisfaction with fellow students

With regard to the first category/code, the students reported mostly of the "red tape" and "thick bureaucracy to penetrate". For example, one student reported as follows:

- The red tape. I don't know if you've heard that or not; just the bureaucracy is so thick; it's hard to cut through sometimes to get one answer about what you need to do, where you need to be. You find out something at the last minute which you should have known three or four months ago. Lack of communication.

With regard to the other category, the students complained mainly about the negative attitudes of some of their fellow students, as was expressed in the words of the following students:

- Negative attitudes and behaviors by other students. Disruptive behavior in the class and the lack of discipline [of students] by professors.

- [Unmotivating] students; may be due to age/maturity level. [View of a non-traditional student].
- The reason? "That's a hard question for me, as far as the motivating is concerned. I'm self-motivated; I'm here because I want to be here. Now, as far as discouraging to me, I have found that there are people here who don't put a lot of effort into their work and don't seem to take things seriously. And that really bothers me because I'm here to learn, and I don't like distractions; but at the same time, that's probably just the age and maturity level [of the students].

A follow-up question inquired whether the students had any feelings of regret having chosen to study at Shaw University. The overwhelming majority of them (almost 98 percent) reported that they had no regrets whatsoever about their choice. For example, one student said:

- Absolutely not. I'm just treated so well; I feel so comfortable. People welcome me as if they know my name; students, faculty, faculty that I've never even known. Maybe I stick out like a sore thumb. I have a positive attitude.

Other students responded as follows:

- I like Shaw, and realize that I am lucky to be in college.
- There is nothing I have found negative here, to be honest. I've always liked Shaw University. I've been very well accepted here.
- I feel I'm treated better than everyone because I am white and because I work here. Also, I think most people assume I work here or I'm an athlete; so I get treated great.

Similarly, when the students were asked if they would recommend Shaw University to a relative or friend, almost all of them(99 percent) said "yes."

Quality of Education at Shaw University

There is a feeling or perception among some people in our country that consider the education provided at HBCUs is not of the quality provided in White colleges and universities. This perception could be traced to the unequal and segregated educational opportunities provided by the nation, in particular prior to the landmark case of Brown v. The Board of Education of Topeka, Kansas in which the United States Supreme Court overturned the Separate but Equal doctrine. The Separate but Equal Doctrine, which supported separate schools for Blacks and Whites, held that both races can acquire an equal quality education if given in separate institutions – ones for Whites and the others for Blacks. The irony of this argument was that the schools were not equally funded and equipped; the White schools obviously got the better of the situation. Jonathan Kozol(1992), in his assessment of the public school system in New York, described the situation as reflecting "Savage inequalities" with respect to the provision of educational opportunities for the children of different racial and ethnic groups.

Again, I refer to my embarrassing encounter with the White students at the university where I was the only Black faculty member and how one student doubted whether I was indeed a faculty member to be accorded the privilege to check out a book overnight. That happened shortly before I came to Shaw University. I was therefore interested in finding out whether the White students at Shaw University felt they were getting as good a quality education as they would expect to have in a White institution. An overwhelming majority of them (95 percent) reported that they were getting a good quality education comparative to one offered elsewhere. In her response to my inquiry one student remarked as follows:

- Most definitely, and then some. Because I know there was an African American man I had worked with previously at a job, and he was complaining about having so much homework that he didn't have enough time to finish it. He was attending NC State [a White school]. I told him I would trade him my homework for his own, and I told him what I had, and he said, "You can keep it."

Only a very small percent (2%) of the students reported that they were not getting the quality of education they thought they would have been getting somewhere else whether at a Black school or White school. For example, one student wrote: "I don't feel as challenged as expected for college, but I don't know if it is because Shaw is a Black School." The issue of quality education is one that can be more thoroughly explored in a larger, comparative study of schools of similar size, type (e.g. public v private), etc.

Unique Learning Experiences Being at Shaw University

With an overwhelmingly Eurocentric K-16 curriculum and pedagogy in the American public school system, White American students were educated to maintain their position of dominance and the privileges (e.g., superior educational opportunities and employment opportunities after college) that came with dominance. Even after the introduction of the multicultural education movement aimed at addressing the evils of a racist education, some of our present day White brothers and sisters still embrace the position of "right" and a perception of superiority over minority group folks. It was against this backdrop that I posed the following questions to the study participants: What unique learning experiences(s) have you had being a student at Shaw University, which you think you may not have had being in a predominantly white school?

Analysis of the students' responses to this open-ended question revealed that, overall, the students acquired some very positive and culturally enriching experiences they thought they may not have had from a predominantly White institution. The following verbatim quotations of some of their responses substantiate this finding:

- I have found my experiences here at Shaw enlightening – culturally and academically.

Another student remarked as follows:

- I think that they taught me that we're all family here, that there is no difference; we're all human beings; we're all here to learn. I've learned that there are still struggles for the African American; that there are a lot of misconceptions; they have to overcome the color issue, the racism, the prejudice. It's hard for them. I'm learning that they're struggling to be understood. That's what I'm trying to understand so that I can help to promote a better understanding of the diversities.

The above responses represent the kind of learning outcomes an instructor, and to a large extent, an institution, would wish for in serving students and the society. These are the learning outcomes (empathy, tolerance, respect and appreciation for difference, etc.) that remain with us long, long after we may have forgotten the mathematics, science, history and the like we learned in school. That's what **real education** is about!

Another student commented about her Shaw University experience as follows:

- I learned what it is like to be a minority. I also looked up and found out more about African American culture than I ever would have at apredominantly white institution. I also learned there are minority scholarships available for white students that attend HBCUs.

The view expressed in the above quotation relating to the stimulation of students to go and search for more knowledge about African American culture reminds me of my experiences teaching about the African American experience in America. For example, in a course titled *Multiculturalism and Globalization,* the first such course to be offered at Shaw University, and which I introduced, and also in my Foundations of Education course, I addressed, in detail, the subject of Black History Month. To many of my White students, the subject of Black History Month presented a new and eye-opening experience to them. For example, they became knowledgeable about why February was chosen to celebrate Black History. Interestingly, even my Black students did to know the reason. Some of them felt February was specifically chosen because it's the shortest month of the year, and that being the case, the celebration would not go on longer than 28 or 29 days. They thought this was all part of the 'racism' to deprive African Americans of knowledge of their cultural roots and contributions to America and the world. In order to prevent this misconception or ignorance to gain ground, I enlightened students, both White and non-whites, that February was chosen to celebrate Black History Month because it coincided with the birthdays of two significant historical figures in American history: President Abraham Lincoln, who signed the Emancipation Declaration abolishing slavery was born on February 12, and Frederick Douglass, the great abolitionist, was born on February 14. It was considered prudent to honor these two important personalities, who were instrumental in fighting for the liberation of enslaved black people, to celebrate Black History Month during the month of their birth.

This is not the kind of information to which Black students, let along their white counterparts, are usually exposed when they study at predominantly white institutions. Another, even more sensitive subject I dealt with in this course related to Rogers' assertion that six of our past presidents were part Black. He detailed this claim in a rare book titled "Black Presidents USA". The shock and surprise with which my students received such information was understandably not surprising to me because they had been kept in the dark for too long. In my Philosophy of Education course I exposed my students, both undergraduate and graduate, to George G.M. James' (1992) book *Stolen Legacy: Greek Philosophy is Stolen Egyptian Philosophy*. In this work, James claims that in fact, the term Greet Philosophy "is a misnomer" (P.1) and that the ancient Egyptians were the authors of the so-called Greek Philosophy and not Greek Philosophers - not even Aristotle, Socrates, Plato, and other Athenian Philosophers to whom, James posited, undue credit has been ascribed for their contributions to the field of philosophy. In fact, James argued that many of the works ascribed to Aristotle were the intellectual property of Egyptian priests which were stolen from the Royal Temples and libraries which the Greeks plundered and pillaged after the invasion by Alexandria the Great (p.1). Another author has written challenging James' claims, arguing that Greek Philosophy did not come from Africa.

The point I want to emphasize here is the importance of exposing our students to as many diverse information as possible. The contents of our lessons must include the popular as well as the unpopular and controversial or ugly. By so doing, we will provide opportunities to our students that will stimulate and encourage them to develop their critical-thinking capacity. The ability to think critically is vital for their proper development as citizens of an increasingly complex, politically and economically volatile, and interdependent world. It would be a great disservice to our students, and consequently to our national development, to hide the truths from them because we feel such truths are sensitive or contrary to the beliefs and comfort of some dominant groups. Our educational institutions should be a marketplace of ideas.

Expressing the benefits he derived as a White student studying at Shaw University, this student wrote:

> I think one of the most important things I have learned at Shaw was the history of African Americans. I have been a jazz programmer for 5 years now and though I have played black music, I never took the time to actually learn where the music came from- the early days at Congo Square in New Orleans, to Chicago, to New York and the Harlem Renaissance. I believe I was placed here by God to strengthen me spiritually and develop a strong relationship with God. With programs such as CASES every Tuesday in the Chapel, I was administered the Word of God through people who lived their lives serving the Lord. In a way I feel that it is my duty to go and get my masters and come back to teach in the Mass Communications Department.

Another student just put it quite bluntly and concisely as follows: "Shaw is the real world." All I can say here about this statement is "what a revelation!" By Shaw being the "real world," I interpret this to mean a real world where people of diverse backgrounds live, learn, and work.

Allyson A. Sesay, Ph.D.

Summary, Suggestions, and Conclusion

Summary

As noted earlier in this chapter, most of the studies that have been conducted in multicultural education or ethnic studies have focused attention on the experiences of minority group students. As founder and executive director of the REACH Center for Multinational and global education, Gary R. Howard (1993), noted: "Most of our work in race relations and multicultural education in the United States has emphasized and appropriately so – particular cultural experience and perspective of black, Asian, Hispanic and American Indian groups." These are the groups who, Howard pointed out, "have been marginalized to varying degrees by the repeated assertion of dominance by Americans of European ancestry" (p. 37).

My study focused on a more unusual situation – experiences and perspectives of a dominant cultural group studying in an environment in which they constituted the minority population. Motivated primarily by my experiences as a minority, in fact, the only Black faculty member working in a predominantly White institution, I investigated the experiences of white students attending a predominantly Black institution. The study revealed important findings about how the educational and life experiences of White students can be enriched appreciably studying in a culturally different environment from their own.

Almost all the students reported positive experiences they acquired studying at Shaw University. Among these experiences were the following:

- The opportunity to acquire an improved understanding of the importance and benefits of studying about and among people of different cultural backgrounds, particularly, African Americans. This was made possible and enhanced by a diverse and friendly faculty who they reported were genuinely interested in their welfare and success.

- A culturally diverse curriculum, particularly, the international studies, diversity and ethnics/values courses.
- No regrets attending Shaw University and will recommend it to other White students to apply.
- Meeting and making friends (friendship that extended and continued outside the classroom) with persons outside their culture.

Suggestions

On the basis of the above and other related findings from the study, I make the following suggestions:

The University should continue to work relentlessly and genuinely to build and promote a culturally diverse as well as culturally pluralistic university community. In this regard, the following points should be significantly important:

- The university should build/capitalize on the students' already acquired positive experiences (e.g. an enriched and diverse curriculum, friendly atmosphere) to enhance and promote cultural pluralism.
- The institution should intensify its efforts to increase racial and ethnic diversity by recruiting more white students.
- The university should actively solicit the assistance of White students in its recruitment efforts to increase the racial/ethnic diversity in the student population.
- In its recruitment efforts the university should provide information on financial assistance available for White students attending an HBCU.
- Instructors should encourage greater, non-politically correct participation in the discussion of issues relating to race and ethnicity. The faculty development office can be of assistance in this respect by organizing diversity training for instructors.

Allyson A. Sesay, Ph.D.

Conclusion

One very important inference one can draw from this study's findings was that Shaw University presents a conducive and facilitating environment in which its White students can feel welcome and comfortable to live and study. Certainly, Shaw's main function at the start was to provide an education for Black students who otherwise would not have been able to acquire an opportunity elsewhere, especially at White colleges and universities in those days. But the institution has always had an unwavering commitment to its founders' mission to provide educational opportunity to students from diverse cultural backgrounds.

The benefits and significance of the student learning outcomes which emanated from the White students' exposure to education and life in a culturally different environment at Shaw University cannot be underestimated. This is the kind of education that is vital to building a truly multicultural and pluralistic American society where all its facets will not just pay lip service to providing freedom, equality, and justice for all its people, but demonstrate, by word and action, a genuine commitment to the realization of this lofty, laudable, and humane objective, which I strongly believe is a moral imperative for any educational institution in particular.

References

Banks, J.A. (1994). An Introduction to Multicultural Education. Boston: Allyn & Beacon.

Howard, G. R. (2003). Whites in multicultural education: Rethinking our role. In J.A. Banks (Ed.) Multicultural Education, transformative knowledge and action (Pp 232-334). New York: Teachers College Press

James, G. G. M. (1992). Stolen legacy: Greek philosophy is stolen Egyptian philosophy. Trenton, New Jersey: African World Press.

Kozol, J. (1992). Savage inequalities: Children in America schools. New York: Harper Perennial.

OSPIRE, Shaw University (2010). Shaw University Fact Book (12th Ed.). Raleigh, N.C.: OSPIRE

Upcraft, M.L. & Stephens, P.S. (2000). Academic advising and today's changing students. In V. Gordon, W. Habley and Associates (Ed.), Academic advising: A comprehensive handbook (pp. 73-83). San Francisco: Jossey-Bass.

CHAPTER 7

Women in the Shaw University Workplace: Perspectives, Successes and Challenges

Introduction

Historically, women have not had as many opportunities for advancing their careers in academe as their male counterparts have had. The ivory tower, which has been traditionally male-dominated, housed a variety of glass ceilings and enclosures that have prevented women from developing their intellectual potentials to the fullest extent. Efforts to advance to higher academic and administrative positions in the academy have usually proven an uphill and sometimes a frustrating battle that have caused many women to abandon their dreams of a career in academe. This situation is true for both White women and women of color. However, Women of color, especially Black women, face a two-pronged problem of inequality on the basis of race/ethnicity and of gender. In his Preface to the famous book *Sisters in the Academy,* in which a group of African American female academics chronicle their experiences in America's Higher Education, Jones (2001) comments as follows:

Despite the fact that there are more female college students than there are males, there is still a disproportionately high number of men who occupy major leadership positions in higher education. Women continue to be critically under-represented in the higher echelons of higher education. For African American women, the numbers are dismal (p. ix).

However, African American women and women in general have made and continue to make appreciable successes in advancing their careers in the academy. Even the very prestigious and oldest institution of higher education in the United States of America, Harvard University, an overwhelmingly male-dominated institution, made history when for the first time in its 371 years of existence in 2007, it appointed a woman as president. There are, however, many challenges females have to face in the nation's higher education.

The purpose of the study on which this chapter is based was to explore the experiences of women at Shaw University, a Historically Black University where the majority of the women faculty and administrators were African American. What were their successes and challenges or perils? The specific objectives investigated are given below.

Specific Objectives of the Study

The study explored the following objectives:

- The representation of women in both academic and key administrative positions.
- Participants' self-evaluation.
- Participants' perception of themselves as role models.
- Experiences participants found interesting/rewarding.
- Experiences participants found not so interesting/rewarding.
- Obstacles to females' career advancement in academe.
- Participants' recommendations to promote gender equity in the academe.

Procedure

Participants

A total of 26 full-time female faculty participated in the study. This number represented about 22 percent of the total population of full-time faculty and 52 percent of the full-time female faculty employed at the university during the time of data collection in 2010-2011. Half (50%) of the participants had worked at the university between 1-5 years; another 22 percent for between 6-10 years; and about 14 percent for over 15 years. More details on the participants are provided in the findings section.

In addition to the faculty questionnaire, I designed and administered, in person, an interview schedule to key university administrators. Using the survey, I analyzed the quantitative and qualitative data generated from both instruments and arrived at the results reported in the findings section presented below.

Findings and Discussion

This study explored essentially the career experiences of female faculty at Shaw University – their level of representation across disciplines, academic rank, and academic administration—factors, among others, that influenced their career advancement. The study came up with important findings that can be used to further enhance the participation of the female members of the Shaw's academy, and, to some extent, shed more light on the situation of women in the American academe, particularly, in this case, with respect to African American women in a Historically Black University.

The findings of the study are presented under the following headings:

- Female representation by rank.
- Female representation in the University administration.
- Female representation by area of specialization.
- Participants' self-evaluation.
- Participants' perception of themselves as role models.

- Experiences participants found interesting/rewarding.
- Experiences participants found not so interesting/rewarding.
- Obstacles to females' career advancement in academe.
- Participants' recommendations to promote gender equity in academe.

Female Representation by Rank

Female faculty have been traditionally known to cluster at the lower ranks of the academe – mainly around the ranks of Assistant Professor and Instructor. Analysis of the data from this study reflected this situation. As can be seen from Table 7.1, 22 of the 36 participants were at these two ranks (42% assistant professor and 19% instructor).

Table 7.1: Female Representation by Rank

Rank	Frequency	Percentage
Full Professor	3	8.33
Associate Professor	5	13.89
Assistant Professor	15	41.67
Instructor	7	19.44
Others	6	16.67
Totals	**36**	**100%**

Females at the higher ranks of the academic ladder – Full Professor and Associate Professor – accounted for only 3 (8.33%) and 5 (13.89%), respectively.

In addition to their academic positions, 33 percent of the participants held academic administrator positions. Table 7.2 shows a breakdown in this regard. There were only one female dean and two departmental chairs as at the time of data collection.

Table 7.2:Females in Academic Administrative Positions

Position	Frequency	Percentage
Dean	1	5.26
Deputy/Assistant Dean	0	0
Chair of Department	2	10.53
Program Coordinator/Director	11	57.89
Others	5	26.32
Totals	**19**	**100%**

The majority of the female academic administrators were directors or coordinators of one program or another.

Females in Key Leadership Positions in the University Administration

In addition to the administrative positions discussed in the previous section (i.e. deans, chairs of department, etc.), I explored the representation of females in key leadership positions at the university's administration positions in which they significantly influence major university policy formulation and implementation. Prominent among this caliber of administrators are the following:

The President: For the first time in 2009, 144 years since the founding of the institution, a female became the Chief Executive. A Spectacular Magazine Cover Story noted as follows: "June, 2009 marked a new beginning at Shaw, when Dr. Yancy became the University's first female president." That historic event took place after 144 years of the institution's existence. "Living up to her reputation," the story went on, "she hit the ground running by immediately reviewing the University's academic programs and analyzing the financial state of the school, in an effort to determine the best possible course of action for eliminating debt and raising the money necessary to take the university into the future." Dr. Yancy did just that and more within her first year in office as evidenced in several very positive statements made during a jam packed Appreciation Day organized by both faculty and staff held in her honor at the University's

Spaulding Gymnasium. One such statement read, "Under the leadership of Dr. Yancy, a manageable level of fiscal strength and stability have been restored at the University." This statement was made against the backdrop of the financial management style of her predecessor's administration.

Vice President for Academic Affairs: Dr. Marilyn Sutton-Haywood became the second female to hold the position of Vice President for Academic Affairs. Her predecessor, Dr. Patricia Ramsey, also a biologist, enhanced research activities at the university.

Vice President for Institutional Advancement: This position has been traditionally held by a female. During the period of this study, Evelyn Leathers was in charge. A major function of this administrator is to help raise funds for the institution.

Vice President for Fiscal Affairs: Again, this is a position held for the first time in the University's history by a female in the person of Debra Latimore. She served as an external auditor to the university prior to her appointment as the Chief Financial Officer. In my interview with her, she revealed she was not accorded the level of respect she deserved as a professional accountant when she was serving as an auditor. Regarding her initial experiences after assuming the position of Vice President for Fiscal Affairs, she told me, "I came here correcting so many things more so dealing with policy and procedures."

The Registrar: The position of Registrar was one of particular interest to me. The Registrar, Ms. Hamilton-Davis, was not only the first female to occupy this position but also the first Caucasian to hold the position. In my interview with her, she told me she had no reservation or hesitation seeking the position when it was advertised, contrary to skepticism some friends and colleagues had expressed when she told them she, a white, was applying. This is another example in which Shaw University had demonstrated a genuine commitment to promoting cultural diversity, namely with respect to gender and race in this particular situation.

The Director of Human Resources: For as long as I can remember, at least for the 15 years I was at Shaw University (and to date), this key unit of the administration has always been headed by a female. However, there is a small difference; as in the case of the university's registrar, the position of Director of Human Resource was held by a Caucasian, another first in the institution's history, here again, demonstrating its genuine commitment to cultural diversity.

Also noteworthy of Shaw University's efforts to appoint women to high-profile positions is the fact that four of the six members of the President's cabinet were women – the president herself, Dr. Sutton-Haywood (VP for Academic Affairs, Debra Latimore (VP for Fiscal Affairs), and Evelyn Leathers (VP for Institutional Advancement). See Figure 7.1 below:

Figure 7.1: Executive Leadership and Cabinet

This is the first time in the university's long history that females have accounted for about 67 percent of the composition of this critically important organ of the institution's administration.

Female Representation by Area of Specialization

I was interested in finding out the representation of females in the various disciplines across the university, but with particular reference to the Science, Technology, Engineering and Mathematics (STEM) fields in which females are traditionally underrepresented, and a field where most of the lucrative jobs of the 21st Century will be found. As can be seen in Table 7.3, the majority of the participants were in the Arts/Humanities and Social Science, representing 20

Table 7.3: Female Representation by Field of Specialization/Employment

Position	Frequency	Percentage
Arts/Humanities	7	20 (14%)
Business	1	2.86 (1%)
Computer Science	1	2.86 (1%)
Education	4	11.43 (8%)
Health/Allied Health	3	8.57 (6%)
Mass Communication	2	5.71 (4%)
Science (Biology, Physics, Chemistry and Environmental Science)	5	14.29 (10%)
Social Science	7	20 (14%)
Visual and Performing Arts	3	8.57 (6%)

Other	2	5.71 (4%)
Totals	**35**	**100%**

Missing case = 1

( ) = Percentages of female faculty at the university at time of data collection

percent each, but only 14 percent each of the total number of 50 female faculty members employed at the university at the time of data collection. These fields, especially Arts and Humanities, are traditionally where many female academics work. Next in size of representation was the field of science, namely biology, chemistry, physics, and environmental science, accounting for 14 percent of the participants and 10 percent of all female faculty. At the time of the study, the chair of the Department of Natural Science and Mathematics which housed the disciplines of biology, chemistry, physics, mathematics and environmental science, was a female, and so was her predecessor, both of them chemists. The Dean of the Faculty of Arts and Science was also a female, the only physics professor and one of the 10 full professors at the university. It is noteworthy that this professor was the first African American female to earn a Ph.D. in physics from North Carolina A and T State University in Greensboro, North Carolina. Females were fairly well represented in the sciences. However, the university should endeavor to attract more females into the STEM fields. For example, there was no female faculty in mathematics, and there were only two in technology – one computer science and the other in instructional technology.

The field of Education, also one in which one finds many female academics, accounted for only a little over 11 percent of the participants and 8 percent of all the female faculty, followed by Health/Allied Health and Visual and Performing Arts, representing about 9 percent each. There was only 1 (1%) faculty in Business and 2 (4%) in Mass Communication.

Participants' Self-Evaluation

Like many other universities, Shaw University evaluates its faculty's performance for promotion on four major criteria – teaching, research, publication, and service.

I was interested in finding out how the participants rated themselves on each of these four criteria. I believe that self-evaluation is an important aspect of work performance appraisal, which, in fact, the Department of Education used in its yearly faculty evaluation. Referring to the case of women in particular, Dwyer and Bruce (1988) note that "how women see themselves and value what they do may in part determine the outcomes they attain."

Using a 5-point scale – 1 being the lowest and 5 the highest – the participants rated themselves on each of the four areas mentioned above. As can be seen from the data presentation in Table 7.4, teaching got the highest rating with about 52 percent of the participants rating themselves "5" and another 39 percent "4." The average rating for teaching was considerably high – 4.32. This was understandable because of the fact that Shaw University is predominantly an undergraduate degree granting liberal arts institution which places a very high premium on teaching – good quality teaching, I must emphasize.

Table 7.4: Participants' Self-evaluation in Teaching, Research, Publication and Service

Area	Ranking					Total	Average
	1	2	3	4	5		Rating
Teaching	3.23%	3.23%	3.23%	38.71%	51.61%		
	1	1	1	12	16	31	4.32
Research	0.00%	21.74%	60.87%	17.39%	0.00%		
	0	5	14	4	0	23	2.96
Publication	42.42%	39.39%	12.12%	3.03%	3.03%		
	14	13	4	1	1	33	1.85
Service	3.45%	13.79%	13.79%	31.03%	37.93%		
	1	4	4	9	11	29	3.86

The next highest rating was for *service*, reflecting about 39 percent of the participants, and an average rating of 3.86. In the area of *research* not even one of the participants rated herself a "5." The highest rating in this category was a "3," representing about 61 percent of the participants. The average rating of this criterion was only 2.96. *Publication* received the lowest rating. This, in essence, means that the women considered themselves to be the weakest or least productive in this area of academics. The average rating in this area was 1.85, with the majority of them, 42 percent and 39 percent, rating themselves "1" and "2," respectively.

In general, the women considered themselves foremost or best in teaching; next in service, followed by research, and lastly, in publication.

Publication and research, it should be noted, carry a very high weighting in an evaluation of faculty performance, especially for promotion. This, in part, explains the underrepresentation of females at the higher academic ranks of the university. It's interesting that the performances that are most related to the university's mission are thought the least important. This situation may explain, in part, the lower representation of females in the higher faculty ranks (i.e. full and associate professors) discussed earlier in the findings. This matter is discussed again later when the participants highlighted the obstacles to their career advancement.

Participants' Perception of Themselves as Role Models

An important positive impact female faculty can have on the female students in an institution such as college or university is the enhancement of the students' self-esteem, a factor critically important for their persistence and success. When students see faculty, especially those in important positions (e.g. Associate and Full Professors, Senior Lecturers, Deans, Department Chairs, and the like), they are likely to be more motivated to aspire to such heights. Such motivation is even more likely when the female faculty serve as academic advisors or mentors to their female students. An item in the participants' questionnaire sought their views on whether they considered themselves as role models at the university, and why. Analysis of their responses showed that as high as 78 percent of them considered themselves as role models for both male and female students. Another 14 percent reported that they considered themselves role models but particularly for their female students. A small percent (8.8) did not consider themselves as role models.

A following question asked: "Why is it important for you to be a role model for female students in particular?" The recurring theme that came out of the text analysis of their responses to this question was that their presence at the university will inspire the female students and give them hope that they too can achieve academic success. The following is a sample of their responses in their own words:

- I came to this university to affect African-American students and our female students need to have guidance to show them the pathways to success.
- Students need to "see" a young African American woman that is a leader within and beyond the academic environment. My students can relate to me on many levels, including ethnicity, socioeconomic status as well as mutual field of study.

I can relate very well to what this faculty (i.e., second question) was expressing, even though from a different but related angle (i.e., race). As noted earlier, I was the only Black at two universities in the state of Maine where I worked. I was a role model for the handful of Black students, in particular for the only African student at the university at the time, and we developed a very close relationship. I became like a big brother or uncle to him, and that contributed in no small way to make life more bearable for him in a very racially and culturally isolated environment. I believe I helped to enhance his academic progress. Another relevant situation comes to mind in this regard. This concerns the situation relating to my daughter while a student of chemical engineering at the University of Maryland at College Park, where the only female professor (also the only African American) in the entire school of Engineering at the time, was looked up to for guidance and support not only by the female students, but also by all the minority students in the male and Caucasian-dominated school.

She took them under her wing and encouraged them to persevere and strive for success.

Another faculty wrote in expressing her reason for wanting to be a role model for her students:

- Because many of our female students struggle being single parents and going to school full time.

In a similar vein another faculty indicated,

- It is important to be a role model for female students because they need someone to look up to while juggling families, full-time jobs, and school.

Another faculty expressed her reason for being a role model thus:

- Because many of our students do not feel as if there is any forward/upward movement available to them.

This faculty explained,

- Female students do not often realize their own strength. They think of female professors as "teachers" and male professors as "professors"; in other words, the power of the position is engendered in gender. Our female students can be positively influenced by examples of authority at least in the academic atmosphere.

Things/Experiences Participants Reported They Found Interesting/Rewarding Working in Academe

Though females have made some significant strides in their careers in academe, there is abundant research evidence, historically and as well as contemporarily, indicating that they have not fared as well as their male counterparts because of discriminatory practices and policies against them.

For example, in the highly illuminating book titled "*Sisters in the Academy: Emergent Black Scholars in Higher Education,* Mobokela and Green (2001) and the various contributors (e.g. Alice C. Collins historical perspectives on Black women in the academy; Mary V. Alfred on success in the Ivory Tower; Gloria D. Thomas on the dual role of women as scholar and change agent; Brenda "BJ" Jarmon's Unwritten Rules of the Game; Rochelle L. Woods' account of her experience as a female ("Invisible females") graduate student at one of the nation's big research universities, etc.) chronicled their trying experiences as they navigated the male- and white-dominated environments of the nation's higher education. Sesay's (2013) exploration of the representation of women in the academy reported similar evidences of the inequity and stereotyping of women, not only in Sierra Leone but globally, too.

In this study I encouraged the participants to tell the stories of their experiences as females in the academy. I do support the view of feminists, in contrast to their anti-feminist counterparts, that allowing women to tell their own stories in their own words about life in academe is crucial to any meaningful discussion on gender equality. It is important, Glazar-Raymo (1999) points out, "To start with women's own experience if we are to understand how profoundly it influences our perspectives, values, attitudes, and role in society" (p.1). Other writers (e.g. Fox-Genovege, 1991, Heilbrun, 1987) have expressed the same sentiment.

From a text analysis of their responses to an open-ended question about what they found particularly interesting and rewarding working in academe, the major theme that emerged centered on students – the joy of influencing and enhancing their academic success, seeing them graduate and going on to graduate school, and becoming successful in their chosen careers. A sample of the participants' responses are reported verbatim in Box 7.1 below (i.e. the things that inspire them in the academy).

Box 7.1: Participants' Views on Things They Found Interesting and Rewarding

- That one student who gets it and excels.
- Learning more about the successes that my students have accomplished.
- When the students finally "get it!!!" that is worth more than gold. Watching them mature… open up like a flower.
- Students' success, the thrill of getting to talk about what I love, great student debates, creative curriculum and interesting peers.
- Working directly with the students and getting to know them as individuals and scholars.
- Seeing the growth of our students. Students push through the program and go on to be successful in doctorate programs or as administrators in the field of ECE (Early Childhood Education) and seeing faculty push to reach their potential.

Things Participants Did Not Find Interesting/ Rewarding in the Academy

As a corollary or follow-up to the previous question, the participants were asked to indicate any particular thing(s) or experience(s) which they found not so interesting or rewarding in their work in academe – especially experiences that border on their being female. Text analysis of their responses provided a variety of views centered around the following themes – gender disparity, the university administration, students, and faculty. Details are provided in Table 7.5. As can be seen from the table, gender disparity was the experience most frequently cited (39% negative).

Table 7.5: Experiences Participants Found Not so Interesting/ Rewarding in Academe

Response	F	%
Gender disparity – workload/faculty responsibilities, salary, sexism	14	38.89

The university administration – not very efficient/supportive	10	27.78
Student – work ethic, respect for authority	5	13.89
Lack of communication among faculty members	3	8.33
Other	4	11.11
Total	**36**	**100.00**

They complained about disparity in the way faculty workload and responsibilities were assigned, sexism, inequity in salary in favor of their male counterparts. One participant put it thus:

"The pay, I believe that a male doing the same job as I do, with the same amount of experience would get more money. I believe that those with less experience get more money as well." However, one participant emphasized that foreign-born females experienced additional inequity in income in addition to that based on gender. She explained as follows:

> There is disparity in income of the Foreign-born females vs. the American-born females with the former earning the least irrespective of qualifications and length of teaching. Foreign-born black women have not made such a gain [in income]. With my Ph.D., I was paid $7,000.00 less than another woman occupying the same position but is an American-born (i.e., an African American).

In a self-consoling manner this academic concluded, "Times have changed for the indigenous African American – and only that cohort. I congratulate them. Our time will come – here, there, right now, some time. This I strongly believe."

One participant, whose response pretty much captured the views of many of her peers, presented a very detailed and a rather emotionally charged comment as shown in Box 7.2 below.

Box 7.2:A Participant Vents Her Feelings/Frustration

There is a great deal of disparity between men and women, male and female faculty here at Shaw. There are different expectations and responsibilities given to female faculty, or assumed they will do. There is the expectation that if you're female, you'll work doubly as hard, or because you're a woman you have a natural instinct to do something deemed "woman's work" or the interest. If you think about it, we have a number of female administrative faculty who are expected to be at everything, participate on every committee, and spend endless hours at Shaw. Male administrative faculty don't seem to get the extra assignments or reports that are unceasingly demanded. For instance, I cannot take a day off during the fall break because of a meeting that could be easily postponed. If a male faculty and staff take on the extracurricular activities of the university – the intimate student involvement. Things like pageants, student government and other organizations are considered "women's work." I cannot name one female faculty member who is an advisor to a student organization. This responsibility also equals financial disparity, as the university does not provide student organizations with financial support. So the simplest of things – refreshment for a meeting, printing, supplies, student materials – becomes out of pocket, unreimbursed expenses that female faculty and staff incur on a regular basis. Again, rarely are any male faculty seen at any activities after 5 p.m. or on weekends, whereas female faculty and staff do this on a regular basis. Generally, male faculty at Shaw does not put in 40 hours + weeks. Students regularly report that they cannot find their advisors. There is also the indirect expectation that female faculty and staff's after hours' time is available especially if they're single. The presence of a male faculty member would have made all of the differences with the large group of students that participated. Women are seen as "mother hens" and their authority is largely ignored. This kind of service, often with endless hours, is not valued as significantly as typical benchmarks like research and community service, which women do not have time to do because they are spending all of their time in direct work with students. One of the things that make me increasingly resentful is the amount of time and

---

energy I put into my students compared to the neglect of my own child, who had been and is often dragged to late night and weekend activities. My own child's development is compared simply due to the lack of my time and attention with a course load of 8 classes, administrative duties, no administrative help, no additional faculty and no university budget, I often feel helpless and I'm constantly frustrated.

It is very hard to dismiss such an expression of inequity with citation of a number of concrete and specific examples contained in the quotation above.

In a similar vein another participant reported as follows:

It seems to me in my department the women tend to be the one who have to do the extra "volunteered" work. The men in the department seem to be able to get by with saying no while we women are expected to kill ourselves out of some sense of duty

Other aspects of the university's administration with which the participants took issue included lots of paperwork, insufficient secretarial/administrative support, and lengthy meetings, as can be seen from the following participants' direct quotations.

- The paper work; lack of administrative/secretarial support, shortage of professors; sexism that's part of culture which comes with exclusive language.
- Dealing with the administration. Nothing to do with gender so far, but if we had much shorter meetings we would get more things done.
- The clique relative to those who are connected through the board members and/or the administration.
- The slow pace of the administration: HR, finance in keeping with research and hiring, and paying on time.
- The system seems to be anti-progressive sometimes. Even though the science department is well funded, we can't always get resource

when we order it. The arms that are supposed to be there to support us, simply by placing an order are the arms that hold us back. It is probably a mere compound question with complicated answers, but I can't seem to wrap my finger around it as yet. In addition, some faculty members do80% of the work, yet it is so hard to get rid of the 20%. It is so puzzling to me how Shaw University does NOT have tenure, yet some professors seem to be tenured in their negligence and disinterest and manage to populate an office around here.

- Not having enough money to do some of the things that I would like to do with the students – like travel, attendance at conferences, facilities not as desirable as I would like.

Some participants (about 14 percent) complained about students, mainly about their work ethic and lack of respect for their authority. One participant commented that "Students sometimes do not show respect and are ready to be confrontational to get their way."

Another participant responded:

"Yes, I would agree to this statement. My experience has been that students are much more likely to challenge my authority in the classroom. I have noticed this among both male and female students."

In a rather frustrating manner another participant wrote:

I can't say that my concerns are related to my gender. Rather, I see a culture at Shaw that does not promote scholarship. This, coupled with a student body that does not prioritize learning, provides a very demoralizing experience. Had I known these things in advance, I would not have taken the job.

Another participant vented similar concerns and frustration in the following quotation:

> This is not an institution that respects its faculty. We are underpaid given the enormous workloads they must face. We are micromanaged, which is very troubling since we are educated individuals. And we are tasked with too many administrative responsibilities that are not normative for many universities. How then, can we be expected to conduct research when we face these enormous responsibilities? And no one, I mean no one recognizes our situations.

It was interesting, eye-opening, mindboggling, but nevertheless, refreshing to learn about some concerns and frustrations these female members of the Shaw academy so vividly expressed. It's only by hearing their voices regarding how they felt about working conditions at the university that steps can be taken to address those concerns more effectively. I was glad I was able to present some of the findings from this study at a faculty forum where the President, the Vice President for Academic Affairs, and other senior administrators were present. It was also gratifying that the President commended me for the study, which implied that something was going to be done to address the issues the participants had raised.

It should be remarked that despite its shortcomings, the majority of the participants in this study regarded Shaw University as a good place to work. As revealed by their responses to the question "would you recommend a female relative or friend to take up a faculty or an administrative position here at Shaw University?", close to 70 percent of them said they would.

In her reason why she would so recommend another female to the university, this participant explained as follows:

> I would definitely recommend working here. I think it is a great place to work. I think all working places come with their unique issues and I can deal with Shaw issues. I

have witnessed both males and females in this department being promoted. It is exciting working under a female administration.

"You have the ability to grow, learn and contribute to continuous growth at Shaw and to African American students at large," another participant reported.

Further analysis of the participants' responses relating to their unfavorable experiences seemed to suggest that their dissatisfaction and frustrations were, in many cases, directed at the administration which Dr. Yancy was called upon to replace in order to spare the institution from what appeared to be an imminent doom, especially financially. Here are some examples of statements made by the participants in support of my theory:

It's exciting to have a female president because it seems like serious issues are being addressed more openly. With previous administrations, the leadership was very paternalistic, much like the doctors who say, "let me worry about that." I like knowing what is happening and what is being done to remedy the problem(s). Also, female leadership tends to be more inclusive (let's all work together) whereas the male leadership has tended to be very paternalistic ("do as I say").

Reacting to the coming of President Yancy, this participant had this to say:

I kind of believe in the current female President. She is a woman of intellect who has achieved. Having studied her disposition a little bit, I think she is a person of justice, who will say exactly what she is thinking so you know where she is coming from and where she is going (that is very, very rare at Shaw University). Usually female bosses can be tough to deal with, but this President has a secured disposition, hence, she tends to be fair. But, I am still studying her. In short, I must say she gives me hope – and

I'm not always this liberal in reviewing female bosses. I have compared her to many in mind and I just had more time to study her – I think she means well to all her employees, and I mean ALL. I may be wrong but I strongly feel that.

Making a kind of comparative analysis of her experience at Shaw University during the Yancy Administration and the one that preceded hers, this academic administrator remarked as follows:

> I do not feel a discrimination toward females now... Under the administration of Dr. __ [I withhold the name] there were times when I felt that the administration did not value my opinion and expertise because I was a woman and also did not value the field of early childhood education and the B-K (Birth through Kindergarten) program.

Similar comments about the Yancy Administration included the following:

- Thank God that she will turn things around.
- Great job she has done. Females can make a difference in the world, if given a chance.

The data from this study did not reveal such complimentary statements about Dr. Yancy's predecessor.

Factors that Militate against Female Advancement in Academe

Several studies (e.g. Omdala, 2013; Sesay, 2013; Rockqwemore, 2008; and Conroy, 2001), have shown that female academics face peculiar problems as they strive to advance their careers in academe in the United States of America and globally. Some of these studies have focused on Black women who face a two-prong problem of discrimination on the basis of race/ethnicity on one hand and of gender on the other.

Other studies (e.g. National Science Foundation, 2008; Etzkowitz, Kemelgor, Neuschatz & Uzzi Kathleen, 1985) have focused on women of all racial and ethnic backgrounds) in specific disciplines such as the STEM fields.

An item on the questionnaire sought the participants' views on factors that are gender-related which affected their advancement in academe. Text analysis of their responses provided a major theme bearing on problems having to do with family responsibilities, including household work, pregnancy and childbearing. As can be seen in Table 7.6, this response represents 62 percent of all the responses.

Table 7.6: Factors that Militated Against Females' Advancement in Academe

Responses	f	%
Spousal/family responsibilities (e.g. pregnancy and childbearing)	18	62.06
Single parenthood and financial obligations	5	17.24
Socio-cultural, political factors/sexism	3	10.34
Others (e.g. lack of role models/mentors)	3	10.34
Total	**29**	**100%**
No response = 7		

In elaborating on her situation in this regard, one of the women wrote:

"I have primary responsibility for 2 children. They are young and so my free time is often spent with them, thereby limiting my commitment to academic pursuit." Another participant explained as follows:

> Having children definitely slowed my progress. Probably being married as well, since my husband has a very demanding job and comes home very late. I do 85% of the parenting and the housework because I am at home early and I am also the expendable one, since my husband's salary is 4 times higher than my Shaw University salary.

In a more detailed and emotional manner, another participant explained:

One of the things that make me increasingly resentful is the amount of time and energy I put into my students compared to the neglect of my own child, who has been and is often dragged to late night and weekend activities. My own child's development is compromised simply due to the lack of my time and attention. With a course load of 8 classes, administrative duties, no administrative help, no additional faculty and no university budget, I often feel helpless and am constantly frustrated. With no resources, I have to devote fully to daily duties. There is no time or energy for research, community service, or professional development. The university doesn't offer opportunities to attend conferences, so keeping current in the field is difficult.

It has been argued that the future career of any married academic woman depends largely on her husband as this relates to childbearing and childcare. For example, a Yale University report on a study in this connection, titled *Report on Childcare: Challenges for Parenting Professors*, several statements documenting the negative impacts of childcare on the females professor were highlighted. The following are some examples of such statements:

Men at all ranks were more likely than women at all ranks to have spouses/partners who worked part-time or not at all, and a higher percentage of men reported that their spouses/partners preferred that condition, findings that suggest that men are more likely than women to have spouses/partners who were available to perform more of the household and child-rearing duties (p.3).

Another important statement was that…

Mothers in academia are disadvantaged by the way we define the ideal worker as someone who can move at will and needs no time off for childbearing or child-rearing. That definition disadvantages women in three basic ways, the most straightforward of which is that most women need time off for childbirth. Most also need time off for child-rearing, Because American women still do the bulk of childcare (p.4).

As a result of this disadvantage and hurdle women face, many of them have been led to feel that "they must choose between parenting and an academic career."

Garson (1985) noted similarly that "It is not surprising that pregnancy and childbearing still have negative consequences for women who work in the United States." However, she noted, the impacts appear to be especially strong in the area of academic science because of its structural features that coincide with fertility.

Also, in regards to women's decision about career choice, Etzowitz, et al. (1994)found that in all the departments they studied a majority of women graduate students indicated that they intended to pursue a career in industry rather than one in academe, since it (industry) was more compatible with family life.

Of those who aspired to careers in academia, the researchers reported, most were interested in jobs in small teaching colleges rather than in research universities because, among other things, they could face the discriminating environment of the research universities. The researchers also pointed out that in academia, especially in the sciences and engineering, a "male model" of academic success prevails, a model that emphasizes "… a total time commitment to scientific work and aggressive competitive relations with peers" (p.12). Women do not usually have as much of the time needed to devote to their scientific work as their male counterparts because of the demand on their time for caring and parenting obligations, as noted earlier.

The authors identified two contrasting categories of women scientists with respect to issues bearing on gender: (1) women who follow the male model mentioned above and who expect other women to do likewise; these are referred to as "instrumentals"; and (2) those who adopt a women's academic model which attempts to combine work and non-academic work (family responsibilities) in a comparative as opposed to a competitive working relationship with their peers. These are referred to as "balancers," with whom the majority of the Shaw University female academics seemed to have identified. Instrumentals are said to behave even more negatively and be less sensitive to the situations or concerns for female students than male faculty who are sensitive to female issues or concerns. Instrumentals, the author rightly noted, cannot be good role models for female students and junior faculty as they attempt to navigate the field of science. The lack of role models and mentors was one of the militating factors to their advancement in academe, the women in this study reported.

Single parenthood, which is closely related to the first factor (i.e. family responsibilities) and financial responsibilities accounted for 17 percent of the responses. For example, one of the participants reported that she had to take up another full-time job (moonlighting) to supplement her Shaw University salary. She explained:

> My full time job (a second job) has affected my progress in the academy. I believe I would have more time to devote to Shaw University if I did not have a full time job, but I need that job to supplement my income from Shaw.

Similarly, another participant noted: "Don't get paid enough to afford baby sitter, and attending some functions to advance my career... such as research and publishing, writing etc."

Socio-cultural and political factors and sexism were also reported to be negative factors in the participants' professional advancement. As one participant put it,

> The social clubs are largely "good old boy clubs." After school socials that involved "downing a beer" didn't always appeal to me. Now that wine is more socially appreciated,

it's added an element of femininity. Progress in research has been largely stunted because I did not always have the personal relationships with veterans in my field of study.

Though men also experience problems in their professional careers in academe (for example, as variously expressed by contributing authors in Lee Jones' (2000) edited book *Brothers of the Academy*, "the lack of social and professional connections available to most women in academic science and engineering departments, in concert with overt and covert gender bias as well as differences in socialization, creates special and unique problems for women" (Etzkowitz, p.3). This lack of social and professional connections notable in academic science and engineering, is also true for women in other disciplines. The "good old boy network" cuts across all disciplines in academe.

Also militating against women's advancement in academe is said to be the lack of political savvy. It is said that "most women are not socialized to understand the political strategies to advancement within the academic system" (Etzkowitz, p.11). This point coupled with other culture conflicts, Etzkowitz and his colleagues noted, discourage many graduate students and young faculty members from pursuing careers at the highest level in academe.

The participants in this study complained about Shaw University being part of the "good old boy" network which excluded women from active participation in policy matters that affect their progress. This criticism was directed not only at the administration but also at the institution's Board of Trustees. This may mean that even when female faculty may be politically savvy, the so-called "good old boy network" may still create obstacles and glass ceilings to their achievement. The lack of male role models to "show women the ropes" on how to navigate academe may further limit the heights to which they can climb. For example, it took the assistance and support of high-level male administrators at the Massachusetts Institute of Technology (MIT) to ensure that one female professor (Nancy Hopkins) successfully fought her case of gender discrimination. Her success became the impetus for other institutions to address and correct similar gender inequality problems.

Participants' Recommendations to Address Gender Equity Issues

In addition to requiring the participants to express their views on gender equity issues at the university, they were also required to recommend possible solutions to help address these issues. Analysis of their responses produced a variety of themes which were merged to further produce the four categories contained in Table 7.7below: Seventy-two percent of the responses fell under the category "Equitable treatment by the university administration." This category represented 72 percent of the responses.

Table 7.7: Participants' Recommendations to Address Gender Equity Issues

Responses	f	%
Equitable treatment by the university administration	26	72.22
Encourage collaboration among the faculty/ membership	5	13.89
Provision of diversity/sensitivity training for male faculty	3	8.33
Others	2	5.56
Total	**36**	**100%**
No response = 7		

Suggested recommendations for the university to effect equitable treatment were

- A more equitable salary structure
- A more equitable work and assignment
- Fairness in hiring and promotion
- Appointment of more women members to the university's Board of Trustees

- Response to issues/allegations of gender inequality raised by female in a timely manner.

The next most frequently cited recommendation (about 14%) was for the university to encourage collaboration among its faculty, and a system where senior male faculty would mentor younger female and male faculty. The participants also recommended that the university provide diversity training for their male counterparts to make them more sensitive to gender issues. Eight percent of the respondents suggested this line of action, and 6 percent gave other recommendations. In Box 7.3 below are verbatim quotations of a sample of the participants' major responses relative to the categories presented in Table 7.7.

Box 7.3: Participants' Recommendations to Address Gender Equity Issues

There needs to be a means to fill in the gender gap in the pay scale. I don't know how to do that… especially since the school is in such a financial bind, but something needs to be done to elevate the pay of women in Shaw.

Have more women on the Board [of Trustees].

Remove 80% of the current trustees; get more administrative support for all departments where needed; make sure women receive equitable pay; provide incentives for research; lower class loads.

Faculties, educational forums, and real mentor program to strengthen young men and women.
Develop Women's Network to meet and document their issues. Mentor new and young women that are hired. Help develop those that are already there. Everyone should be privy to in-service training opportunities. Meet with the men and discuss how all could be great team members. Men and women can work together successfully for a cause of educating all students and ensuring your place of work is the best. Attitude is the key in getting the job done. STAY POSITIVE.

The first need is to provide a more equitable work load. There needs to be some consideration of people's humanity. My life is NOT Shaw University! However, it consumes everything ... my sleep when I wake up in the middle of the night going through the never ending list of tasks; the last minute calls to do something over the weekend or during the evenings; the demands for time sheets as if we're all imbeciles or dishonest. We need to be honest with each other. The men (particularly faculty) just say they're not going to do something, or just ignore requests. The women make sacrifices to do something, often out of fear of losing their jobs.

Diversity training for the male faculty members. Since many of the male faculty members are from other cultures, many carry different views of women which create tensions with their female colleagues.

Hire/promote a person based on his/her capacity not on his/her gender/race.

Management should be upfront at all times. They should address issues immediately. They should respond to allegations/suggestions with the same enthusiasm [for males as well as females]. They should assign appropriate weights to complaints.

Administration needs to look at all the salaries and adjust the income of those that have been put on the back burner. Check at least the degrees and length of service along with the income. They will find a lot of disparity.

The leaders of the institution and the Alums need to work at this very sticky issue.

Summary, Suggestions and Conclusion

This study explored the career experiences of female faculty at Shaw University – their level of representation across disciplines and academic ranks, and academic administration; and factors that influenced their career advancement, among others. The study came up with important findings that can be used to inform policy formulation on the female members of the Shaw academy, and to some extent, shed some more light on the situation of women in the American academe in general, and particularly, in this case, with respect to African American women in one of the nation's Historically Black College/University (HBCU)!

In terms of their representation in the various disciplines in which the university offered instruction, females were fairly well represented, especially in the arts, social science, and education, which is atypical across the nation. There was, again, as is common across the nation, low representation in the STEM fields. Females fared well in their representation in key administrative positions: the Registrar, Director of Human Resource, Director of Faculty Development, for example, were all females. The President's Cabinet consisted of four females, including the President, out of the six members.

In the area of academic ranks, the majority of the female faculty clustered in the ranks of Assistant Professor and Instructor, with very few in the Full Professor and Association Professor ranks. Related to this finding was the participants' self-ranking of themselves in the area of Teaching, Research/Publication, and Community Service. The majority of them rated themselves higher in Teaching and Community Service than in Research/Publication, which is a criterion rated highly in an evaluation for promotion to senior faculty ranks – Associate and Full Professor.

Among the major factors which the participants reported as militating against their career advancement were unfair workload assignment (curricular and extra-curricular), family and child-bearing responsibilities, poor and inequitable salary structure, and lack of mentorship for junior faculty. However, despite these negative influences, most of the participants expressed positive views about their overall experience in the Shaw academe. An overwhelming majority of them indicated they would recommend a female relative or friend to take up employment at the university. Expressing her view for both male and female members of the university to work collaboratively, one participant noted as follows:

"We can work together – NO MAN OR WOMAN IS AN ISLAND and NEITHER STAND ALONE." The findings in general indicated that faculty morale, as a function of President Yancy's administrative position and performance, was good at the time of data collection.

One thing I would have loved to do in this study was to hear the voices or perspectives of a sample of the male members of the university, particularly on issues on gender inequity, regarding, for example, their views on salary, workload, and the female members' criticism about Shaw exhibiting the "Old Boy Network" syndrome. I do hope that future researchers on this thorny issue of gender inequality in the academy will provide an opportunity for a comparative analysis of both the female and male faculty members' perceptions of the most salient issues on this subject.

In light of the major findings from the study, I offer the following suggestion for Shaw University Administration to try the following:

Provide a mentorship program in which senior faculty (both male and female) will mentor their junior colleagues. A major focus of such a program should be assisting female faculty to improve their productivity in the areas of research and publication, the area in which the study participants ranked themselves the lowest. Such a mentoring program could be housed in the university's Faculty Development Unit.

- Investigate the matter of alleged unfairness in the allocation of responsibilities, especially the additional extra-curricular-related and after-school assignments.
- Provide some specific grants (may be mini-grants) geared specifically to enhance female faculty members scholarly productivity.
- Start early to recruit and nurture future female academics, especially in the STEM fields. Provide incentives (e.g. scholarships, grants, work study in the STEM and other female underrepresented fields) to high school students, and undergraduates.
- Shaw students Alumni Association and other private organizations should be encouraged to donate monies to such a venture mentioned above.

- Investigate the charge of unfairness in treatment of Shaw University's culturally diverse faculty, especially with respect to ethnicity, religion, and national origin. Just as the university considers it important to offer training on the subject of sexual harassment, every year there is a necessity to provide similar training in cultural diversity as a way of enhancing cultural pluralism, for the existence of cultural diversity in an organization does not automatically produce cultural pluralism in which persons of diverse cultural background live and work side by side, sharing and respecting each other's cultural background.

It is my belief, judging not only from findings from this study but also from my personal experience during my 15-year sojourn, that Shaw University will continue to improve the lives of its female members as well as that of every member so that it will continue to live up to its motto Pro Christo et Humanitate (For Christ and Humanity).

I would like to conclude this chapter on women on a light-hearted note, with the following quotes by some of the world's great ladies:

The phrase "working mother" is redundant.

Jane Sellman – University professor and writing consultant at University of Maryland School of Nursing.

A man's got to do what a man's got to do. A woman must do what he can't.

Rhonda Hansome – African-American actress, popularly known for her role in Pretty Woman in1990 and 8:46 in 2011.

Whatever women must do they must do twice as well as men to do though half as good. Luckily, this is not difficult.

Charlotte Whitton – (1896-1975)A Canadian feminist; Mayor of Ottawa; the first female mayor of a major city; founding Director of the

Canadian Council on Child Welfare, now the Canadian Council on Social Development.

Behind every successful man is a surprised woman.

Maryon Pearson – (1901-1989) – was wife of Lester Bowles, the 14th Prime Minister of Canada. Popular for her famous quotes.

When women are depressed they either eat or go shopping. Men invade another country.

Elayne Boosler – Comedian, writer, political activist, animal activist.

In politics, if you want anything said, ask a man. If you want anything done, ask a woman.

Margaret Thatcher – Nicknamed the Iron Lady, became leader of Britain's Conservative Party in 1979 and elected Britain's first female Prime Minister that year and governed till 1990.

I have yet to hear a man ask for advice on how to combine marriage and career.

Gloria Steinem – American feminist, journalist, author, and social and political activist

A male gynecologist is like an auto mechanic who never owned a car.

Carrie Snow – Famous American stand-up comedian and comic writer.

Laugh and the world laughs with you. Cry and you cry with your girlfriends.

Laurie Kuslansky, Ph. D. Expert Jury Consultant.

> I am a marvelous housekeeper. Every time
> I leave a man, I keep his house.

ZsaZsa Gabor – An Hungarian-born American socialite and actress.

> Nobody can make you feel inferior without your permission

Eleanor Roosevelt – Wife of 4-term US President Franklin D. Roosevelt and the longest serving First Lady – 1933-1945.

- Brief bios retrieved from www.yahoo.com search engine

References

Alfred, M.V. (2001). Success in the Ivory Tower: In Mabokela and Green A.L. (Eds). Sterling, Virginia: Stylus Publishing LLC.

Collins, A.C. (2001). Black Women In The Academy: An Historical Overview.

Etzkowitz, H, Kemelgor, C, Neuschatz, M. &Uzzi, B. (1994). Barriers to women in academic science and engineering. In Willie Pearson Jr. and Irwin Fechter (Eds.). Who will Do Science? Educating the Next Generation. Baltimore: Johns Hopkins University Press.

Fox-Genovese, E. (1991). Feminism without illusion: A critique of individualism. Chapel Hill: University of North Carolina Press.

Gerson, K. (1985). Hard choices: How Women Decide about Work, Career and Motherhood. Berkeley: University of California Press.

Glazer-Raymore, J.C. (1999). Shattering the Myths: Women in Academe. Baltimore: Johns Hopkins University Press.

Heilbrun, C. (1988). Writing a woman's life. New York: Ballantine Books.

Jamon, B. "BJ" (2001). Unwritten rules of the game. In Mabokela R.O. & Green, A.L.

Jones, L. (2000). Brothers of the Academe: Up and Coming Black Scholars Earning Our Way in Higher Education. Sterling, Virginia: Stylus Publishing, LLC.

National Science Board. *Science and Engineering Indicators 2008.* Arlington, VA. National Science Foundation, 2008.

Sesay, A.A. (2013). Continental and diasporic African women in the academy: A case for scholarly collaboration. In Falola, T. &Teboh, B. (Eds). The Power of Gender The Gender of Power: Women's Labor, Rights, and Responsibilities in Africa. Trenton, N.J.: African World Press

Thomas G.D. (2001). The dual role of scholar and social change agent: Reflections from tenured African American and Latina faculty. In Mabokela R.O. & Green, A.L.

Woods R.L. (2001). Invisible women: The Experiences of Black Female Doctoral Students at The University of Michigan. In Mabokela R.O. & Green, A.L.

CHAPTER 8
Special Recognition and Gratitude

In my acknowledgement I mentioned some persons who assisted me in one way or another to put this work together. There are also many other fine folks with whom I sojourned at Shaw University, and among these are some very special ones who deserved my special thanks and gratitude for their collegiality and unwavering support at various times as I labored in the Shaw University vineyard for 15 years. I want to spend the next several pages of this book to register my profound appreciation and gratitude to them for their support in making my time at this great and historic institution a rewarding experience both personally and professionally. This special recognition goes to the following persons:

- ❖ Mr. Sama Mondeh
- ❖ Dr. Collie Coleman
- ❖ Dr. Talbert O. Shaw
- ❖ Dr. Vernice Loveless
- ❖ Dr. Lillie Boyd
- ❖ Dr. EmekaEmekauwa
- ❖ Dr. Patricia Ramsey
- ❖ Dr. Joan D. Barrax

- ❖ Dr. Ademola L. Ejire
- ❖ Dr. Deloris Jerman
- ❖ Dr. Sheik U. Kamarah
- ❖ Dr. Charles Tita
- ❖ Mr. SahrGbondo
- ❖ Mr. Brian Cumberbach
- ❖ Mrs. Sharon Joseph
- ❖ Mrs. Bessie Lewis
- ❖ Mrs. Gwendolyn Starr
- ❖ Mrs. Linda Stephens
- ❖ Dr. Marilyn Sutton-Haywood
- ❖ Dr. Dorothy C. Yancy

The order in which the persons above are listed does not in any way reflect their importance to me or the level and amount of assistance they offered. Rather, they are listed and discussed more on the basis of, pretty much, the order in which I met them when I arrived at the university, than on anything else.

MR. SAMA MONDEH

I got to know about Shaw University through Mr. Sama Mondeh, then the Vice President for Fiscal Affairs. He had heard me talk about the trying situation associated with my being away from my family living in Maryland while I worked way up in Northern Maine. One day he called me and inquired whether I would be interested in a position that had opened up at Shaw University. My response was, "Is the Pope Catholic?" A few days later I got a call from the Vice President for Academic Affairs regarding the vacancy – Director of the CAPE in Fayetteville, North Carolina. In addition to letting me in on the job at Shaw University, Mr. Mondeh took me in with his family (room and board free) for a month. I also rode with him to and from work during this period, and on several occasions I rode with him on weekends to Maryland to see my family. I also remember our lunch at the Fish Market in Raleigh, where we enjoyed good sea food and comradeship.

For these opportunities and hospitality I remain eternally grateful to you. Your wife, Grace, also deserve my gratitude for her understanding and hospitality to me during my month's stay with your family.

DR. COLLIE COLEMAN

I first met this energetic, fast-paced moving, open-minded, and astute administrator when he called me on the phone while I was at the University of Maine at Fort Kent (UMFK). He wanted to have a preliminary interview with me regarding the position I was seeking at Shaw University where he was serving as the Vice President for Academic Affairs. Dr. Coleman struck me as a friendly, genuine gentleman. But he was also very crafty, getting me to tell him exactly what I was being paid at UMFK in his second or third sentence during our brief telephone conversation. Someone had told me not to disclose my exact salary during a job interview, for it would be improbable for me to be offered a salary much above the one I disclosed. Did I learn a lesson from my salary-negotiating experience (if, in fact I can call it a negotiating experience) with Dr. Coleman? I ended up being offered the exact salary I was making at UMFK even though I had argued about Raleigh, North Carolina's higher cost of living than Fort Kent, Maine's to justify my request for a higher salary.

Anyway, despite my losing the salary negotiation "game" with Dr. Coleman, he became one of my greatest sources of support, assisting me to settle down as a newcomer to not only the University but to the city of Raleigh and the state as a whole. I remember to this day a promise which he made to me as I was leaving his office on my way to be introduced to the chair, faculty, and staff of the Department of Education for the first time. He said to me, in confidence, "I know you are not going to find it easy over there [i.e. in the Department of Education] because you are not from here [i.e. an American], but the Administration will be solidly behind you." He never faltered on this promise! He supported my application for funding to attend several professional conferences which contributed in no small way to enhancing my professional career. Importantly also, he was instrumental in my getting appointed the chair of the then Department of Multidisciplinary Studies (MDS) two years after my arrival at the university. By virtue of that appointment I became a member of important university-wide committees, including the Strategic Planning Committee. The experiences which I acquired serving on these committees have proven and continue to prove very rewarding in my professional growth. I had been Head of Department at University of Sokoto, Nigeria, but serving in this capacity at Shaw University provided me a different dimension to educational administration and management, especially adjusting to cultural differences that impacted my leadership role.

As a result of our close professional and cordial personal relationship with Dr. Coleman, two of my colleagues – Dr. Sheikh Kamarah and Dr. Charles Tita – and I became known as the *Coleman Boys.* I guess – in fact, I believe – that because of Dr. Coleman's positive experience living and working as a Peace Corp volunteer in a couple of countries in Africa, he developed a special liking for the three of us – Dr. Kamarah and I from Sierra Leone, and Dr. Tita from Cameroon. Also, importantly, and I say this with great pride, Dr. Coleman took keen interest in us because of our competence, congenial work ethic, and an unwavering support for the university administration headed by a very committed, dynamic, and selfless President, Dr. Talbert O. Shaw. I am proud to have been dubbed a Coleman Boy.

Thank you, Dr. Coleman, for all your support, and may your soul continue to rest in perfect and everlasting peace.

DR. TALBERT O. SHAW

After my interview with Dr. Coleman I was taken over to meet with President Shaw. The first thing that struck and impressed me was the cleanliness and orderliness of his office which matched his elegant and captivating presence. He reminded me of two important adages I had learned in grade school many years back – "cleanliness is next to godliness" and "order is the first law in heaven." This is one man, I said to myself, who personifies the teachings of his vocation – the Clergy.

Dr. Shaw welcomed me with an urbanity that made me feel comfortable and relaxed. He started his conversation by telling me about his growing up on the family farm as a young boy in Jamaica. He told me about how he used to wake up early in the morning, walk to the farm to do some farm work, and return home to get ready for school every day. I did not grow on a farm like Dr. Shaw, but I could identify with the story of his boyhood in Jamaica. We shared similar other experiences. Growing up in Sierra Leone, West Africa, I walked miles to and from school as Dr. Shaw did and performed domestic chores for my parents on a daily basis before and after school.

After about 15-20 minutes of our going down cultural memory lane, our conversation shifted to the main purpose of our meeting – to discuss the position I was seeking at the University. He started by commenting on how impressed he was with my CV, and wasted no time to offer me the position as follows: "Well gentleman, the position is yours if you want it." I replied in the affirmative and thanked him for the offer. "You will like it here; it's a good place to work," he assured me. With that, we parted company, and he promised me that I was going to get a formal letter of offer within a week's time.

Honestly, though I was excited about the prospect of working at Shaw University, especially when I thought of the possibility of not returning to cold and far-off Maine, I was not too keen to become a CAPE Director at Fayetteville, North Carolina. For one thing my family was not going to relocate to North Carolina. They were pretty much settled in Maryland, where my children (Ola and Sammy) were actively involved in track and field at school (at Roosevelt High School) and in the local club competitions for the Chillum Striders and the Glenarden Track Clubs.

In addition, my wife loved her job with the Holy Cross Hospital in Silver Spring, Maryland. Relocating my family was therefore out of the question. Also, for a Director of a CAPE program, Saturday operation was a must, because this was when many students (mainly adult working students) could more comfortably take their classes. With such a situation it was going to be difficult for me to visit my family on weekends and to be in a position, among other things, to travel with my children to their many track and field competitions across the entire country. Do I turn down the offer at Shaw, or do I take it at the expense of being away from my family on most weekends and miss out on the opportunity to go and support my children in their athletic performances?

Also very importantly, taking the CAPE Director position was not going to avail me the opportunity to teach education courses, which were not offered at the CAPE locations. That was going to drastically reduce my active engagement in my discipline and intellectual home of education. The thought of that saddened me, to put it lightly.

If I decided to turn down the offer, it would avail me the opportunity to spend more time with my family but without the income and benefit package Shaw was going to offer me. I was thus like between a rock and a hot place.

As a Christian, I prayed fervently for God's guidance in making a wise decision. Lo and behold, my prayer was answered. When I received the letter of offer from Dr. Shaw, it stated that because of my expertise and many years of experience in the field of education at home and abroad, the university had decided to offer me a faculty position in the Department of Education and the then Department of International Studies with the former as my primary department and the latter as my secondary. When I read the letter I screamed with joy, so loud that my wife and children heard me from the basement. "Yes! Yes! Yes," I continued to scream until my folks joined me to find out the reason for my unusual emotional outburst. I just handed over the letter to my wife for her to discover the good news that I was no longer going to Fayetteville. What an emotional relief that was for my entire family. I thank God for His blessing and immediately called Dr. Shaw and thanked him for his decision to change my appointment.

The impact of Dr. Shaw's decision to offer me a faculty position on the Raleigh Campus instead of the CAPE directorship in Fayetteville has been profound on both my professional and personal development. The following are but a few examples in this regard:

- As a 9-month faculty (instead of 12-month as CAPE Director), I had the whole of my summers free to do as I saw fit. Immediately after turning in my final exam grades at the end of the spring semester in May, I was off to Maryland to spend the entire summer with my family and return to Shaw a day or two before the start of the new academic year in August. This made it possible for me to take my two athletic children (Ola and Sammy) to track and field practices three days each week while my wife went to work on the night shift. I was also able to travel with the kids to their local, regional, and national competitions. This was tough and very demanding of our time and financial resources (e.g. club registration fees, uniforms, traveling and hotel expenses, etc.) over a ten-year period. However, the "sacrifice" paid off big time: Both Ola and Sammy went on to university (Sammy at George Manson University in Fairfax, Virginia and Ola first to the University of Kentucky, Louisville and to the University of North Carolina at Chapel Hill) on full athletic scholarship. These are top-ranked and costly universities which would have been difficult for us to afford for our kids' education without the financial aid which the athletic scholarships provided. Also importantly, by being able to be with the kids at practice and their trips to cheer them in their competitions, we developed a strong bond with them.
- As a full-time faculty in Education and International Studies, I became more actively involved in teaching and research than, I am convinced, I would have been able to do in the position of a CAPE Director. Also, I became Chair of the then Department of Multidiscipline Studies, a position I may not likely to have been offered from the CAPE directorship position. The Chair position opened up many opportunities that helped enhance my career development. For example, I designed some new courses that were taken by students in both the main campus and CAPE locations. I became much more actively involved in my area of specialism, Education, than I would have if I had been at the CAPE program in Fayetteville.

A very important quality of President Dr. Shaw was his genuine concern for his members of the Shaw Family – faculty, administrators, staff, and students. Each time I met him, whether in his office or as he walked across campus, he was very gracious and would ask me about how I was faring and also about my family.

Dr. Shaw was also very cognizant and appreciative of one's contribution to Shaw University, an institution he loved dearly. His comments on my autographed copy of his book "The Renaissance Years at Shaw University" attests to his recognition of my contributions to the university. That's one of my psychic incomes I discussed in Chapter 9. That meant a lot to me, especially for my moral. In my opinion, faculty moral has never been as great at Shaw University since the departure of Dr. Shaw in 2002.

While in the Department of Multidisciplinary Studies, Dr. Shaw, at my invitation, came to my class and delivered a guest lecture on the topic "Religion and its impact on the Human Condition." This was for a course I had designed entitled "The Human Condition: A Global Perspective" in which we examined how various factors (e.g. economics, race/racism, gender, health, religion, etc.) impacted the human condition worldwide.

Dr. Shaw's lecture was not only well received by the students, it also provided an opportunity for many of them to meet and speak with him in person for the very first time.

Another episode in my sojourning at Shaw University and for which I owe gratitude to Dr. Shaw happened during my very first semester at the institution. As I mentioned earlier in this chapter, the position I initially applied for was as the Director of CAPE in Fayetteville, but Dr. Shaw and, I imagined in consultation with the then Vice President for Academic Affairs, Dr. Coleman, decided to use my talent and experience in the Departments of Education, and International Studies. This decision to assign me to these departments was made administratively. I did not go through the usual hiring/recruitment process, and because of this, I was not well received in the Department of Education, to put it mildly. I therefore wasted no time to embark on a frantic job search. Luckily, after a grueling search process, starting with a total of 95 applicants, I ended getting a faculty position in Education at Eastern Kentucky University in Richmond, Kentucky. The salary offered was much higher than that which Shaw University had offered me and so was the benefits package. With such an enticing offer and the opportunity to walk away from what I considered a hostile work environment in the Department of Education at Shaw University, I was ready to pack my bags and say goodbye. However, out of decency and respect for Dr. Shaw, I arranged to meet with him before making my exit from the university.

During my meeting with President Shaw, I explained the reason for my decision to first of all seek another position elsewhere and why I had decided to leave after only a semester at the institution he had said was a good place to work. He listened to me uninterruptedly while I explained my case. In an emotional tone he made the following statements to me, which made me change my mind about leaving the university, a decision I never regretted. He said "Don't go. Stay here. I'm telling you in confidence, my Africans are my best people here." That was a deep and telling statement to come from the Chief Administrator. We shook hands, I thanked him, and I went to the Department of Education with an iron-clad resolve to not let anything or anyone whatsoever stand in the way of getting my work done to the best of my ability as a professional educator and decent and God-fearing human being. That was the beginning of 15 years of a successful sojourning at historic Shaw University.

Thank you, Dr. Shaw, for encouraging me not to quit Shaw University and for the many ways you supported me during our years together at this great institution which you loved and cherished so much, and which you literally raised from near collapse to a position of financial buoyancy and sound academic integrity. I am proud to have been a small part of that history made possible because of you.

God bless you as you continue to enjoy your well-deserved retirement.

DR. VERNICE LOVELESS

Dr. Loveless soon became my friend, colleague, and sister upon my arrival in the Department of Education. I mentioned earlier about the lukewarm welcome that I was accorded when I first joined the department and how I had almost left after only a semester. Well, Dr. Loveless was the only one who warmly welcomed me into the department. I was assigned one of her courses – *Teacher as a Facilitator of Learning*, which was one of her favorite courses. Working together on this course, which had a field experience component that she helped me organize, brought us closer together. We had a great working relationship and her wonderful husband, Leroy, became a personal friend of mine. Leroy, I still take your favorite drink Jack Daniels, to which you introduced me, but unlike you, I blend it with coke before consumption to keep me warm during the cold weather.

Thank you, my friend, for making life comfortable for me at a time when it seemed so cold and culturally exclusive. God bless!

DR. LILLIE BOYD

I first met this veracious and highly talented and assiduous academic and astute administrator when in 1999 I was appointed the Chair of Department of Multidisciplinary Studies. One of my major responsibilities was to develop the strategic plan for my department. As a newcomer to the university's planning business, I needed some help in putting my plan together, and I wasted no time to call on Dr. Boyd, then the Special Assistant to the President and head of the Office of Strategic Planning, Institutional Research and Effectiveness (OSPIRE). She not only consented enthusiastically to help but walked all the way from her office to my department to work with me. The hour and a half we spent together in the International Studies Center (ISC) conference room provided me an improved understanding of the tools and mechanisms of designing a strategic plan (one-year and 5-year) for my department. As a member of the university's Strategic Planning Committee, I continued to learn from Dr. Boyd.

In addition to her planning competence, I admired Dr. Boyd's no-nonsense approach to her work. Our strategic planning meetings were highly well planned, focused and devoid of the kinds of unnecessary digressions I witnessed at some other meetings I used to attend at the university. Behind that smiling face and boisterous laugh was an "iron lady" who took full charge and control of the crucially important business of running OSPIRE. Her exemplary leadership of the self-study helped in no small way to get the university successfully through the re-affirmation of accreditation exercise conducted by the Southern Association of Colleges and Schools (SACS) in 2002 for a 10-year period.

It was a pleasure indeed working with this fine scholar and administrator, a proud alumna of Duke University about which she always bragged. My encounter with Dr. Boyd provided invaluable learning experiences for me, experiences that have proved and I am sure will continue to prove very helpful to me in my professional career as well as in my personal life.

Thanks a lot, Dr. Boyd, for all your assistance and for your genuine collegiality and friendship.

DR. EMEKA EMEKAUWA

Dr. Emekauwa was the Deputy Vice President for Academic Affairs when I joined the university. It did not take time for us to bond after Dr. Coleman had introduced me to him. He soon became not only my senior colleague but also a true brother and friend. He offered me very useful professional and personal advice that contributed to my sojourn in The Shaw University academic vineyard, sometimes a challenging one, but nonetheless peaceful, fulfilling, and enriching.

Two statements which Dr. Emekauwa made to me at critical moments during my sojourning at Shaw University have remained with me over the years. I have drawn from these statements with success in times of difficulty and uncertainty. He made these statements to me on two occasions. The first was when he was leading me to the Department of Education, at the request of his boss, Dr. Collie Coleman. He recounted to me a powerful statement President Shaw had emphasized during his very first meeting with the faculty, administrators, and staff upon his assumption of office. "I don't want to hear the word 'foreigner' here because we are all foreigners," Dr. Shaw warned. Dr. Emekauwa advised me to always remember the statement and to rest assured that I will be fine at Shaw University with Dr. Shaw as its leader. I believed him, and it turned out to be one of the most valuable pieces of advice I ever received from a colleague at the university.

In another situation when Dr. Emakauwa had just lost his position of Deputy Vice President for Academic Affairs due to a change in Administration, he humbly accepted a lower and less visible position at the university's radio station. In a discussion with him shortly after this change in rank, we philosophized about life and work, and he said, "Sesay, in life no condition is permanent." Though that was not the first time I had heard that profound statement, it, for a reason I could not figure out, resonated with me in a special way as never had before and it made me reflect on its meaning more deeply than I had ever done. The reflection and introspection I had gave me a new perspective on my sojourning at Shaw University and to some extent, on my personal life as a w hole. Also, Dr. Emekauwa's statement was kind of prophetic because not too long after there was a change in administration due largely to maladministration which reversed considerately the great gains Dr. Shaw's administration had striven so hard to achieve.

Thank you Dr. Emakauwa for being such a great and true colleague, brother, and friend.

Lest I forget, I thank you also for assigning to me the portfolios the CAPE students submitted for evaluation for the award of credit for experiential learning. The assignment brought in some "change" that helped with the bills.

DR. PATRICIA RAMSEY

Dr. Patricia Ramsay, the first female Vice President for Academic Affairs appointed during Dr. Shaw's tenure, worked with great vigor to promote scholarship, especially grant proposal writing and scholarly presentations at professional conferences among Shaw University's faculty. I took advantage of the opportunities and encouragement she provided in this regard. I wrote and received funding for some research projects through the Faculty Development Office that she established. For the years she spent at the university she funded in full at least one scholarly conference trip (sometimes two) which enabled me to present papers at professional conferences. This helped to enhance my visibility in the academy at the state, regional, national and international levels, and the impact of such endeavors on my career advancement cannot be underestimated.

Thanks also for her morale support. I remember one specific case in point in this regard. I was presenting a report on a research I had conducted on females in academe at Shaw University and St. Augustine's College at our monthly Faculty Forum. One colleague stood up and asked in a condescending and angry voice "Why are you doing research on women? We all know there is disparity." What a strange and unscholarly question I thought that was, especially coming from an academic, for even now as I write several years after my study, the investigation into gender disparity in the academy still continues. Dr. Ramsey, who was chairing the forum came to my rescue and made the following kind of sarcastic remark in response to my colleague's remarks: "At least somebody is doing research." Thanks for that statement. It comforted me and I hope it made my colleague reexamine his position and embark on some action research in his field – philosophy and religion.

DR. JOAN D. BARRAX

I came to Shaw University when Dr. Barrax was leaving to join the administration of Chaney State University as their Provost. I heard very good things about her administrative leadership ability and work ethic. One of her distinguished achievements at Shaw University was successfully taking it through the rigorous accreditation exercise of the Southern Association for the Accreditation of Colleges and Schools (SACS). She was the first to accomplish this task for the university. A senior colleague who had served under her at Shaw University told me she was a strict and demanding boss but also fair. "I thought this lady wanted me out of this place because she kept sending me job advertisements from various other colleges and universities. But when I had the opportunity to see the performance evaluation she had written for me, I was shocked because it was damn good. I developed an open respect for her" this colleague told me in an emotional voice. Another colleague and a fine scholar, who has had appreciable success in grant proposal writing, told me this about Dr. Barrax: "She is very demanding and will work you to death, but I have not regretted it. Most of what I know about grant-writing I learned from her."

So, when I met Dr. Barrax upon her return to the university in 2002, I had a fairly good idea of the kind of "boss" and leader I was going to work with. She came in as the new chair of the Department of Education which was experiencing a leadership problem. Between 1997 when I joined the university and the time of her arrival to the department in 2002 the department had had five chairs – yes, five different chairs. Just five years with her combination of a democratic and sometimes authoritarian leadership style, a "no nonsense" approach to work, and what I call a "freak for documentation" the department was again on an even keel and right on course for another successful re-accreditation by the NCDPI and NCATE, a feat we accomplished with flying colors in 2004, just two years after her arrival.

During the years I worked with this fine scholar, astute and assiduous leader, I learned quite a bit from her and grew professionally as a result. Her uncompromising attention to detail, here focused approach to chairing our very long department meetings (we had a lot to cover in keeping with ever-changing accreditation requirements form NCDPI and NCATE) were key elements of Dr. Barrax's work ethic I admired and incorporated into my own work with positive dividends.

For the first time in the history of the university Dr. Barrax introduced the position of Coordinator of Academic Advising and Volunteer Service, a position which I gladly and enthusiastically accepted. This position opened up a number of opportunities for my professional growth. Documenting academic advisement activities and the volunteer services provided by faculty and staff across the university provided me a new orientation and approach to planning and administration. Also, because of my academic advisement responsibilities, I became a member of the esteemed National Academic Advising Association (NACADA), a great organization that provides support and training for academic advisors through its publications, workshops, and regional and national conferences.

As the Coordinator of Academic Advising and Volunteer Service, I became actively involved in the activities of NACADA, especially attending the annual conferences and presenting papers based on my research studies on academic advising at the university. As can be seen from the Table of Content of this book three of the ten chapters have dealt with the subject of academic advising. I also wrote an academic advising handbook for the Department of Education and designed an instrument for documenting faculty and staff volunteer services to the public schools. These activities and accomplishments have contributed in enhancing and enriching my curriculum vitae and which consequently opened up rewarding opportunities for me. These included the Teaching Excellence Award, positive reviews of my performance by the Dean of the College of Graduate and Professional Studies and the Chair of Education, my promotion to a Full Professor and to some extent, I believe, my Fulbright Award in 2010 – 2011 academic year. I owe much of this to Dr. Barrax who offered me the position of Coordinator of Academic Advising and Volunteer Services.

Also importantly the position increased my salary significantly. Though the university administration did not approve the salary she had recommended for the position, what I received improved my earning quite appreciably. When I moved from the position of Chair of Multidisciplinary Studies to a teaching position in Education, my contract changed from 12 months to 9-months with a considerable drop in salary. The Coordinator position brought me to a 10-month contract with a sizeable salary differential from what I was hitherto making as a 9-month faculty. For this and other assistance including the wonderful letters of support for my application for promotion to full Professor and for the Fulbright Award, I will be eternally grateful to this great scholar, administrator, and wonderful human being called Joan D. Barrax. She is quite a great dancer too, I must add. I will always remember how she was "getting down" at the departmental Christmas party held at my home.

God bless you my friend and continue to enjoy your well-earned retirement.

PROFESSOR ADEMOLA L. EJIRE

Professor Ejire was one of the first faculty colleagues that captured my attention and admiration for his scholarly achievements as well as his outgoing personality and humanity. We soon became buddies when I got to the university in 1997 and we have remained professional and personal friends since then. He was my go-to colleague and brother on a number of occasions when I had to make some critical professional decisions and his wise advice had always helped my situation. I had very few friends when I first got to Raleigh, North Carolina. My family then lived in Maryland.

I appreciated your invitation to your home, especially at Commencement Day when you hosted a grand lunch for your graduates and close friends. I always looked forward to that occasion to feast and more importantly to enjoy fellowship with colleagues and friends from across campus and the university community. Thanks also for the boxes of books in biology and environmental science which I have donated to colleagues in Sierra Leone.

I learned recently that you have left the services of Shaw University. What a loss of a dedicated, loyal and unwavering supporter of Shaw University and its community!

I thank you also for serving on my Promotion Committee when I applied for Full Professorship. At a dinner I had at our home in Raleigh to celebrate the occasion of my promotion you made a statement that has remained engraved in my memory and which has ever since (five years ago now) aroused in me a strong feeling of pride and great accomplishment. You said, "Since I have been here at Shaw University I had never seen a portfolio so well put together as Dr. Sesay's and I said there is no way this man is going to be denied his promotion." Whenever I looked at that portfolio which indeed I painstakingly put together for many months, I always reflected on your profound and motivating statement. The feeling that follows is always sobering and heartwarming.

Thanks my brother, for all your help and your friendship during the years of my sojourning at an institution we loved, and I know you continue to love even though you have made your exit from there. God bless!

DR. DELORIS JERMAN

Life in the workplace can be hectic and challenging, but nevertheless exciting and rewarding. On the other hand, life can be unmotivating, stressful, and unfulfilling. Both these conditions or outcomes can be influenced to a significant extent by the type of boss or leader the workplace has. A supportive and inspiring leader produces the latter outcome which is needed for enhancing productivity in the workplace. I was lucky to have had a boss and colleague in the Department of Education at Shaw University who possessed these supporting and inspiring attributes – Dr. Deloris Jerman, to be specific. Having been groomed herself by a boss with whom she served as Department Chair and Deputy Dean, she had acquired impressive leadership skills and work ethics. Like her boss, she also exhibited the characteristics of a "freak" for documentation, which was actually good for our Department of Education where scrupulous documentation of everything we did was needed in our ongoing preparation for re-accreditation by NCDPI and NCATE, and for SACS, too. Working with Dr. Jerman helped in enhancing my skills in documentation and organization and these skills have proven invaluable in my professional career as well as in my personal life.

Another very important way Dr. Jerman influenced my career, and consequently, my personal life as well was her encouragement for me to apply for promotion to Full Professor. I was contemplating on first completing some projects I was pursuing before putting in my application for promotion, but Dr. Jerman in her wisdom and thorough familiarity with my professional activities and accomplishments insisted that it was time for me to apply. As then Chair of the Department of Education she wasted no time to constitute my Promotion Committee and wrote me a detailed, 3-page single-spaced letter of support. Sometimes I would go back and read her letter of recommendation and each time I did, I would have goose bumps as I admired her candor in detailing my accomplishments and contributions to the department. One part of her letter was particularly humbling and touching to me – she wrote "Much more could be written about Dr. Sesay's work at Shaw University. He is truly a role model for all of us. His accomplishments are numerous, as evidenced in his portfolio. After reviewing the portfolio, I feel you will agree that he is the perfect candidate for academic promotion to the rank of Professor." The statement that I was a role model for my colleagues, including the departmental chair, Dr. Jerman, herself, was particularly revealing and humbling. I never knew I had had such an impact on my colleagues.

Thank you Dr. Jerman for all your support and friendship. Your advice for me to not postpone my application for the rank of Full Professor paid off big time. Apart from the prestige that accompanied the promotion, the financial gain by way of increase in salary would have been delayed at least for one whole year if I had postponed my application. May God Almighty continue to bless and keep you in sound body and mind.

DR. SHEIKH U. KAMARAH

Dr. Kamarah was one of the first persons I met when I got to Shaw University. He welcomed me to his home with an uncommon hospitality. It did not take long for us to develop a true friendship and brotherhood. Thanks, Sheikh for the many delicious meals we shared at your home and for the good times we shared reminiscing about life in our beloved homeland, Sierra Leone. I always looked forward to our visits which made my life in Raleigh a little more exciting.

I thank you also for your assistance in getting me my first apartment at the Green Castle in North Raleigh where you introduced me to another Sierra Leonean, in fact, a former student of mine at the Government Boys' Secondary School in Magburaka, Sierra Leone. This young man,

AlieuWurie, was then a faculty in Chemistry at a sister college – St. Augustine's, there in Raleigh. I was so proud of this young man's academic accomplishments, including a Master's degree in Chemical Engineering. With Alieu, my circle of friends began to grow gradually and I started feeling more and more at home in Raleigh.

Another thing I have always liked about Dr. Kamarah's personality is his love for life, how he goes about life with an uncommon, unfazed calmness, and his insatiable love for cracking jokes sometimes even when one approaches him with what one thinks is a serious matter. He would first find or create something funny about the matter, laugh over it, before giving you his perspective or advice as the case may be. One such situation comes to mind: During my very first semester I had constructed my final exams and showed them to Dr. Kamarah for his feedback. To my surprise he burst out laughing after reading two or three of my essay questions. Jokingly he said in our lingua franca, *"Bra, if na dem kain kwestion ya yu wan bring na ya, na kot os dem go ker yu"* meaning, if these are the kinds of questions you are going to give here, you will be heading to court, I guest to defend myself for using a lethal "academic weapon" to inflict undue pain on my students. I got my friend's message and warning! What he was warning against was not to be too demanding in my assessment, given the overall caliber of students we were dealing with at the university, many of whom would find the quality of question I had prepared difficult even just to comprehend. I took Dr. Kamarah's advice seriously, amended my questions (not watering them down, though) and had no problems from then on.

Lest I forget, it was a pleasure being one of the "Coleman Boys" with you.

You were going to get me in a faculty position at Virginia State University where you work currently, but divine providence dictated that I should remain at Shaw University for which I have no regret.

Thanks my brother for all your assistance and friendship to making my sojourning at Shaw University a pleasant and fruitful one.

DR. CHARLES TITA

After a month's stay with Mr. Sama Mondeh when I first moved to North Carolina, I shared an apartment with Dr. Charles Tita, whom I fondly called Charlie. In Charlie's apartment we had no shortage of African cuisine. I brought my Sierra Leonean dishes from Maryland and he prepared his delicious very tasty Cameroonian meals. This brother is a great cook. Staying together with Dr. Tita was quite fulfilling, professionally and personally. Our discussions always revolved around academic matters at the university, social and political events; and we loved and appreciated the same kinds of music.

When I moved into my own apartment having our meals together did not end. At least three days out of our five-day work week we had lunch together – mostly at Ten Ten, a Chinese Restaurant, and at another popular spot at Cameron Village in Raleigh. Sometimes we would pull some other colleagues to join us. Boy, did we have a good and relaxing time? After the usually heavy buffet at Ten Ten I would go home after work and could not eat. Irene would say kind of angrily "I know you were out eating with Dr. Tita." She always loves for me to eat a big portion of her delicious dishes.

Thanks, Brother Tita, for your friendship and collegiality during our years at historic Shaw University, especially during the Talbert O. Shaw and Collie Coleman era. I am glad to have been as you were one of the so-called "Coleman Boys". Lest I forget, Fellowshipping with you at Davies Street Presbyterian Church in Raleigh to which you introduced me was also spiritually fulfilling.

MR. SAHR GBONDO

This young man is not only a highly knowledgeable and skilled computer specialist, but also very respectful and always willing to give assistance to anyone in need. Sahr, as he is popularly known in the university community, was one of the first few Shaw employees I got to know upon my arrival in Raleigh. He introduced me to Mr. Charles Tita which led our becoming apartment mates as I've mentioned. Sahr made sure I got to know all the important places including the Motor Vehicle Administration, competent and honest auto repair shops, and shopping centers where I could get the best deals. He also introduced me to his personal physician whom I kept till I left North Carolina.

With regard my professional career, Sahr contributed quite a bit to facilitate my growth. If it was assistance in understanding a new software (e.g. Jenzabar) for registration of my students, turning in my course grades, providing me with research data, shopping for new technology, Sahr saved me many a misstep. Sahr also came to my home to help me fix problems with my computer or to set up a new computer outfit I had acquired. The amazing thing about Sahr's personality was that he rendered all this assistance willingly and graciously. He epitomizes the biblical adage "to give and not to count the loss or ask for a reward."

A very important instance I will never forget was Sahr's assistance in completing the 2010-2011 Fulbright Application (online) which I had worked on so hard over several months. After his regular work hours he put in time to ensure that my application was successfully submitted. That was a big relief, to say the least, and to crown it all my Fulbright Application was approved, an accomplishment which is a major highlight of my professional career. Thank you, Sahr, for your assistance in making this accomplishment possible.

I want to thank you also, Sahr, for your assistance, first of all in getting me a very reliable shipper, and for the many hours you spent with me and my family packing up our personal effects and loading them into a 40-foot container for shipment to Sierra Leone in preparation for my relocation.

Sahr, I know you have always admired me genuinely for my children's educational and career accomplishments. Well, my friend, I pray that your children, Sahr and Tamba (and maybe more to come) will be as successful as or even more successful than mine so that you will retire as a proud father as I am. With your impeccable work ethic and your unconditional love for your family, the future holds great blessings for you and your family. Thanks for all your help and friendship. May God bless you and your family with sound body and mind and great prosperity.

MR. BRIANCUMBERBACH

This quiet, coolheaded gentleman who is very competent at what he does in data generation and analysis in OSPIRE, was my "go-to-person" whenever I needed data for several of my research studies, including some of those reported in this book. Also, long before the introduction of the instructional software, Blackboard, and recently Moodle, I administered tests to my students using scantron. This made scoring of tests for large classes in particular easier and faster. Again I would call on Brain for help in this regard, and he willingly responded to my request with dispatch. Whether I met him in person in his busy office, which I did on many occasions, or just sent him an email of my request, Brian always came through for me.

Brian, you contributed appreciably to help facilitate my work during the years of my sojourning at Shaw University, and for this I will always remember you with a great sense of appreciation and gratitude. We are both die-hard Washington Redskin fans despite the winning drought that has plagued us over the past several years. But we are bouncing back; the draught is coming to an end and once again, in the not too-distant future we will be jubilant again as we were in 1982 Super Bowl Champions. Let's just hang in there, brother! Go skins!

Once again, thanks for all your assistance and may God continue to bless you as you strive to help make Shaw University the best it can be.

MRS. SHARON JOSEPH

With a full-time teaching load, administrative responsibilities including writing reports, a busy research agenda, and preparation for conference presentations, among other tasks, I was many times overwhelmed as I tried to cope with the myriad of demands of my work at Shaw University. On many occasions I had to seek help from outside my department whose administrative assistants and secretaries were almost always overwhelmed with large volumes of technical work. One person I could count on for help was Mrs. Sharon Joseph, the then Administrative Assistant to the Director of Faculty Development. Whether it was help with typing exam questions, conference papers, or other documents, Mrs. Joseph never at any time turned down my request, even when at times I had to ask at the eleventh hour. In order to avoid using university time to do my work, she would take it home or stay over after work. Her work was of high quality and her computer skills were second to none in my book.

Of all the many tasks Mrs. Joseph did for me, one that stands out and for which I will be eternally grateful was her assistance in putting together my portfolio when I was applying for promotion to the rank of Full Professor. Even though I had put a lot of time and talent collecting the many folios I needed to produce a good quality portfolio, her special and professional touch to the organization of the work resulted in a very impressive product which elicited a strong positive evaluative remarks from my promotion committee chair, Professor Ejire I alluded to earlier in the chapter. It's a product I am always proud to show off, and I owe you, Mrs. Joseph, a ton of gratitude for your assistance in facilitating such a remarkable accomplishment in my professional career.

Thank you again, Mrs. Joseph, for your valuable assistance which contributed in making my sojourning at the Shaw University academic vineyard a very rewarding and memorable one. God Bless!

MRS. BESSIE LEWIS

I first met this quiet soft-spoken and assiduous worker and snappy dresser when she was serving as Administrative Assistant in the Humanities Department, chaired by my friend, Dr. Charles Tita. I will always remember the many lunches we had together with Dr. Tita and the fruitful discussions we had as we enjoyed our meal. I always looked forward to those times when we "fellowshipped" together. When Mrs. Lewis moved to the Academic Affairs Office, she provided me information for my research projects as well as other pertinent information to facilitate my sojourning at the university. I will remember our professional association and friendship for a long time.

MRS. GWENDOLYN STARR

This very kind, efficient, and highly professional Administrative Assistant came to my aid in desperate times, especially when I needed a conference paper typed. She gave of her time and talent willingly and graciously, and with that infectious smile she always wore. Gwen, I thought I had gotten rid of that "British S" but coming back home to Sierra Leone, a former British Colony, I'm picking it up again. I know you will laugh loudly when you read this. God bless, my friend, for your assistance in facilitating my work at Shaw University.

MRS. LINDA STEPHENS

I know when she reads this piece about her she will feel flattered, shake her head, and smile, or even laugh. As the only Administrative Assistant in a very busy professional department (teacher preparation), Mrs. Stephens has always carried a colossal workload – documenting the department's activities in keeping with the demands of the NCDPI and NCATE accreditation requirements, typing reports, answering unending telephone calls, supervision of work-study students, running errands, among many other duties, Mrs. Stephens, nevertheless, always found time for me, more so towards the end of the first semester in November/December. As I prepared to travel home to Sierra Leone for the Christmas vacation, I was usually under great pressure to get all my work together in order to be able to check out of the department before the close of the semester. Checking out of the Department of Education was a colossal task, with a check-out list a page long requiring documentation of grading of exams and turning in the results, doing the detailed teacher-made test report for each course taught, academic advisement during the semester, analysis of students' work products, etc. As the department Coordinator of Academic Advising, I had the added responsibility to ensure that all students' folders were up to date, including verification that each one of them had been advised at least twice during the semester. During these tensed periods, I usually had to leave the country a little early before the end of the semester so as to get at least three full weeks of vacation time considering the cost of the air fare of over $2,000 and traveling time of four days to and from Sierra Leone. Mrs. Stephens often came to my help, especially going through my advisees' folders. "Don't worry Dr. Sesay, I take care of you," she would say in her soft and graceful voice. These kind gestures made a whole lot of difference in enabling me to travel home to spend Christmas with my extended family. And while I was away in Sierra Leone, Mrs. Stephens made sure mail, especially my desk copies of books from publishing copies were well secured.

For the above mentioned assistance and support to me, I will forever be grateful to this diligent, very polite, warm, and friendly colleague who gave of her time and expertise willingly and asked for no reward. God bless you Linda Stephens.

DR. MARILYN SUTTON-HAYWOOD

Sometimes it is not so much the material rewards in terms of money, clothes, jewelry, and the like that we offer to others that have impact to raise their morale and motivate them to become more productive and loyal to an organization. Rather, it is the little, apparently insignificant things we do and say that may have a more lasting influence in inspiring others. Dr. Sutton-Haywood, Vice President for Academic Affairs, did just that to me during one of our monthly Faculty Forums. I was making a presentation on one of my research studies. With the microphone in one hand, I moved back and forth from the corner of the stage where the laptop was placed to the center of the podium to change and discuss my PowerPoint slides. Seeing this strenuous for me, Dr. Sutton-Haywood said to me in her gentle soft voice, "Don't worry Dr. Sesay; just go ahead and do the presentation. I'll change the slides for you," and she kept changing the slides for me until I completed my presentation. Dr. Sutton-Haywood, that gesture which you may consider not a big deal was a big deal to me. If for nothing else, it demonstrated that you were interested in and appreciated what I was doing. It has been three years since this incident, but it still remains fresh in my mind and I am not likely to ever forget it. Thanks, for coming to my help. I know many a high-ranking administrator may have felt "too important" to change slides for me. I am so happy you are not one of those for Shaw University does not need them.

DR. DOROTHY C. YANCY

Like Dr. Sutton-Haywood, Dr. Yancy made just a short simple statement to me that lifted my spirit and made me feel respected and appreciated. After the presentation mentioned above involving Dr. Sutton-Haywood, and another presentation, Dr. Yancy commented to me, "I liked and enjoyed your presentation." I could feel the genuineness in her voice as she uttered this motivating and morale-boosting statement. You cannot imagine how proud I felt to have been commended by the University's chief executive, herself an accomplished academic.

I want to take this opportunity to thank you also for approving my Sabbatical leave less than a year after your arrival at Shaw University. I enjoyed our meeting in your office in which you told me about your vision and plans for the historic institution of which you became its first female president. I wish you the very best as you lead Shaw University to another successful re-affirmation of accreditation by SACS. I sometimes wonder what shape the university would have been in today if you had not stepped in to rescue it from its impending doom due to inept and unscrupulous administration and management, especially, financial. May God bless and keep you in sound body and mind.

I would be remiss not to mention, even in passing, my family members in the Department of Education who helped make our department a place I always enjoyed going to every working day: The charming, easy-going, and effective Chair, Paula Moten-Tolsen, my sister in Christ, Lucy Wilson, Melvin Wallace, Juanita Linton, Joyce Richardson, and not forgetting the many fine intelligent and assiduous work-study students. We were really a team from heaven. You know what I mean, my friends. I thank you all for your camaraderie and support. I wish you another successful re-accreditation by NCDPI, NCATE, and SACS.

Lest I forget, my thanks go also to the many security officers I met and had the pleasure to work with over my 15 years at Shaw University. I thank them especially for responding promptly to my calls for them to let me into the Department of Education in the Talbert O. Shaw Building on weekends, including Sunday mornings, and on some public holidays. I needed to get to my office at these quiet times to do many of the tasks that have helped me acquire the level of success at the university. I could tell from the looks on their faces that they probably must have been asking themselves something like "My goodness, doesn't this man have something else to do on weekends and holidays than come to Shaw?" Nevertheless, they always responded to my calls with dispatch, grace, and impressive professionalism. May God bless you all, my friends, as you continue to keep Shaw University a safe place to work and study.

CHAPTER 9

A Bank of Psychic Incomes

Monetary income is undeniably of great value to a worker, for among other things, it helps pay the bills – rent/mortgage, food, clothing, medicine, entertainment, education, and other essentials. God has blessed me quite abundantly with this type of income since I started working after high school. There is, however, another type of income, which one cannot use to pay one's bills but which, nevertheless, provides one a sense of personal satisfaction and fulfillment, especially knowing that one has made a difference in another person's life or development. This is what is referred to as *psychic income*, and I can boast of a fat bank account of this type of income acquired during my professional life as a teacher and college professor, including my 15 years spent sojourning in the Shaw University academic vineyard. With no intention to brag or be ostentatious, I am going to share a sampling of my many psychic incomes from students, my faculty colleagues, and administrators from the university. I am going to present them in their exact words, verbatim, many of them expressed in greeting/thank you cards, some in letters of recommendations/support, and others and in Email messages. The incomes are presented under the following headings:

- Incomes from Students
- Incomes from Faculty Colleagues
- Incomes from Administrators

INCOMES FROM STUDENTS

Mrs. Gwendolyn F. Starr
35 Clover Court
Franklinton, NC 27525
(919) 494-2256
gstarr@shawu.edu

March 27, 2006

Dr. Grace Ndip, Chair
FDAC
Shaw University
118 E. South Street
Raleigh, NC 27601

Dear Dr. Ndip:

This correspondence will serve as my official recommendation that Dr. Allyson Sesay, Professor, receive the prestigious honor, Teaching Excellence Award. My recommendation is based on the following:

Fall 2005, I was a student in Dr. Sesay's class, Foundations of Education. Dr. Sesay was professional, knowledgeable, approachable, and injected tasteful humor. He was always well prepared to teach and provided helpful and constructive feedback in a timely fashion.

He was not only a teacher, but his professional role often transformed into motivator, and counselor as he went above and beyond providing helpful literature which provided the class in-depth knowledge on a given subject and/or issue(s).

I feel competent to divulge deeper into the field of education because Dr. Sesay has set the pace in which I can achieve my goal—to one day become a high school English teacher.

My peers often reflect on the class we took under Dr. Sesay and know that we are better prepared to take advanced educational courses because of the guidance and pacing of Dr. Sesay.

In times like these, Dr. Sesay represents "a new Shaw for a new millennium" and I am proud to have studied under his leadership. He is a role model for other professors to emulate.

Sincerely,

Mrs. Gwendolyn Starr, Student
Teacher Certification - English

Comment: *I am flattered but thanks, anyway, Gwen! It was a pleasure having you in my class – mature, intelligent and sophisticated*

12308 Penrose Trail
Raleigh, NC 27614
(919) 488-7900
March 29, 2006

Dr. Grace Ndip
Faculty Coordinator
Shaw University
118 East South Street
Raleigh NC 27601

Dear Dr. Ndip:

It is with honor that I am writing to recommend Dr. Alyson Sesay for the Teaching Excellence Award at Shaw University.

I had Dr. Sesay as a professor in Foundations of Education in my first semester at Shaw University. Dr. Sesay taught in an interesting and informative manner. I was returning to college after 17 years in the workforce and spending time at home raising my two children. After deciding to enter the teaching field, I enrolled in Shaw University. I will admit to having been anxious about my decision. Dr. Sesay has been an awesome professor and mentor to me. He has been encouraging and demanding. I have enjoyed attending his class and hope to be able to take another of his courses. I have attended other courses at Shaw and have not seen other professors take control of their classrooms as Dr. Sesay has. In many of my classes students use their cell phones and enter late. Dr. Sesay stated his expectations at the beginning of the course and kept the class on topic and did not let this be a disruption, therefore, class time is used for learning the subject matter.

I have also gained vast knowledge in the area of diversity from Dr. Sesay. When I began working in an elementary school in downtown Raleigh, I quickly recognized that I needed training in teaching diverse students. Dr. Sesay was very helpful in this area. In Foundations of Education, we spent a great deal of class time discussing diversity within the classroom and community. As the only white person in the classroom, I was able to begin to relate to situations that I have never experienced before. Dr. Sesay has a love of teaching and a goal of making the teaching profession a better place.

I recommend Dr. Sesay for the Teaching Excellence Award at Shaw University without any hesitation.

Comment: *Glad I could help, especially in the area of multiculturalism/diversity.*

Sincerely,

Pamela J. Foster

180

Sesay, Allyson

Thanks for all your help during this course. It was and always will be appreciated. A lot of what you said and what was discussed in class turned into assignments for my students. Most of which they enjoyed.

One last question: When will grades be posted? I need to turn a grade

One last question: When will grades be posted? I need to turn a grade.

But thanks again. I will look for more courses with you in the future.

john kilsheimer

From: Sesay, Allyson [mailto:asesay@SHAWU.EDU]
Sent: Mon 5/7/2007 8:26 PM
To: Kilsheimer, John
Subject: RE: Foundations of Education

John:

I have just made the exam available again on blackboard. It will remain posted till 11:00 A.M. tomorrow, May 8, 2007.

Dr. Sesay

From: Kilsheimer, John
Sent: Monday, May 07, 2007 8:10 PM
To: Sesay, Allyson
Subject: RE: Foundations of Education

The issue I had with Blackboard is that I am not a Shaw student. I am taking your course through the NC Model Education Teacher Collaborative. I received my Blackboard password and PIN the two hours before the test closed out. So I need the 2nd test reposted or if that is an issue forgive the zero in your grade book (wishful thinking). But I don't want to get a poor grade in the class for a technology issue.

My phone number is 252.642.4322 (anytime).

Thanks

John kilsheimer

From: Sesay, Allyson [mailto:asesay@SHAWU.EDU]
Sent: Wed 4/25/2007 2:36 PM
To: Kilsheimer, John
Subject: RE: Foundations of Education

John:

I can understand your frustration with the technology problems we have been encountering. It's frustrating for me too. Anyway, why did it take you so long to get your "Pin #" for blackboard? Like I told you in class a couple of weeks ago, your username is your school ID. # and your password is your pin #, both of which you should have gotten when you registered for class at the beginning of the semester.

I may decide to repost the test on blackboard for you, but I feel obligated to extend this opportunity to others who could not take the test on time.
7/11/2007

Comment: *Showing understanding to and exercising patience with students can pay off in improved student morale, academic performance, and persistence.*

Sesay, Allyson

From: Juanitalinton@aol.com
Sent: Sunday, April 27, 2003 2:35 PM
To: Sesay, Allyson
Subject: Re: (no subject)

I received your message. Thanks alot. I will complete exam and email it to you by Friday, 5/2/03.

I really enjoyed your class and thanks a million for everything.

Juanita

Comment: A *word of appreciation such as the one above warms the teacher's heart. Juanita was taking a master's course from me when she wrote the comment above and she has almost completed her doctoral degree in education.*

May 3, 2002

Just a little note of thanks right from the heart!

Dear Sir
It has been a pleasure meeting you. My wish for you is _all_ the best. May God Bless you and your family.
Thank for everything.
Sincerely,

Comment: *An ambitious but frightened non-traditional student who needed just some encouragement and understanding. Glad I was able to help!*

... in essay,

Thank you for everything especially teaching me about multiculturalism. You will always be remembered!

Comment: *Multiculturalism/ multicultural education is my cup of coffee, and I am happy I was able to win some "disciples" such as Ms. Lowe.*

Thank you!

Sincerely,
Saunjrah Lowe

19 August 2000

Dr. Sesay,

Thank you so much for your reference and support in me getting into graduate school. I have been formally accepted into North Carolina State University Graduate School of Education. I attended both sun sessions and I am proud to tell you that I made the dean's list.

Again, thank you for your help. I will keep in touch.

God bless,

Zoa Murray

Comment: *Teaching and academic advising go beyond the classroom. I'm happy I was able to not only teach and advise Ms. Murray, a busy non-traditional student and parent, but also to assist her get into graduate school. She has earned her doctorate degree. I knew she will go places the first time she walked into my class. It pays to combine academic advising and teaching, as demonstrated by Ms. Murray's success*

Comment: Showing understanding to a student's personal life problems can go a long way to enhance the academic advising relationship between advisee and advisor. I'm glad I was able to help Beverly cope with her problem and was able to complete the semester successfully.

Your kindness
meant a lot...

"May the LORD repay you for what you have done.
May you be richly rewarded by the LORD..."
RUTH 2:12 NIV

Comment: *You said it all, my friend! That's what it takes to help a student get through college even during some trying times.*

... *Thank you very, very much!*

Dr. Josay,
I would like to thank you very much for
bareing with me this semester during very hard
times. Thank you for being understanding, kind,
and caring. I really appreciate everything you've
done to help during this hardship.
Thank you for your words of encouragement, that
... Thank you deeply,

You might think
that what you did
was a little thing
because you do so much
for others all the time,
but it is rare to find
people as considerate
and thoughtful as you.

To: Dr. Sesay
From:- Lorna Lewis.

Thank you for being so
patient with me in Class

Comment: *Patience is a great attribute of a teacher. It can do wonders for your students and for you, too. Thanks, Lorna, for thanking me for what I enjoy doing – teaching and advising.*

5 **Gideon Recognition**

Bibles *have been donated*

IN HONOR OF YOUR

Gracious help and kindness

These Bibles were provided by

Sharon Duke

ADDRESS *231 Gentry Ridge Road*

CITY/STATE *Roxboro, NC*   ZIP *27573*

"But the word of the Lord
endureth forever"
I PETER 1:25

Comment: *Thanks for the
kind gesture, Ms. Duke. Your
donation of a Bible on my behalf
will enable many more to read
the words of God. I'm glad I was
able to help.*

Dr. Essay,

Thank you for such a beautiful card. I read it over and over again; it was very nice that you took time to give your graduates a special word. Also, thank you for being a very thorough and considerate advisor.

You are a great scholar and I am honored

Thanks for remembering my graduation.

To have something (of great depth) that you've written.

May God Bless and Take Care of you.

Ann Harm

Comment:
A testimony that the empirical law of effect works – reinforcing students' effort enhances learning. Glad I was able to help.

Dr. Sesay

I want to Thank You
so much from the bottom
of my heart for all of
your support and encouragement during my time
at Shaw University. I
want you to know that
it meant a lot to me
to have professors that
care and wanted me
to succeed. you will be
greatly missed. Again
I want to express my
humble gratitude
THANK YOU
Lucy

Comment:
*I'm flattered, Lucy, but thanks
all the same. Glad I was able to
help.*

191

Allyson A. Sesay, Ph.D.

Another category of psychic income

Another example of psychic income from my students which I continue to cherish as I reflect on my work at Shaw University was the JOY and PERSONAL SATISFACTION I experienced watching my students from my *Foundations of Education course* deliver their papers at state-wide undergraduate research conferences, especially the annual SOARS (Seizing Opportunities for Advancing Research Scholars) conferences organized by North Carolina Central University in Durham, North Carolina, with sponsorship from the North Carolina Consortium on Undergraduate Research. It used to take quite a bit of convincing and cajoling of the students to get them to accept the challenge to go and make an academic presentation, especially at another university away from their familiar campus setting. Those students did so much pride to themselves and Shaw University by their expert Power Point presentations and confident reactions to questions not only from their peers but faculty supervisors from other colleges and universities across the state. However, there was one particular conference that brought me the greatest accomplishment and psychic income of them all. This was another undergraduate conference organized and hosted by the University of North Carolina at Greenville, North Carolina. This one was particularly awesome because the researchers I mentored for that conference consisted of a group of **First Semester (2011/2012) freshmen** students from my Freshman Studies course. Their composure, self-confidence, and stellar presentation impressed the audience of their peers and faculty members from various institutions, both private and public, across the state. Unfortunately, I retired from Shaw University shortly after that year and did not have the opportunity of continuing to nurture those highly talented and motivated young men and women. I hope someone else is continuing this effort of exposing undergraduate students to take part in research and make presentations outside their comfort zones this early in their academic life. Mentoring and nurturing the researchers of the future must start early, even at the high school level.

INCOMES FROM FACULTY COLLEAGUES

November13, 2007

Dr. Deloris Jerman, Chair
Department of Education
Shaw University

Re: Recommendation for promotion

Dear Dr. Jerman:

It is a real pleasure for me to have the opportunity to recommend for promotion someone of good heart, great talents, and superb work ethics. I was privileged to serve as a faculty member under Dr. Sesay, when he was the Chairperson of the Multidisciplinary Studies Department. The very short two years we worked together, I strongly believe, will go down in history as one of the most productive experiences I have had at Shaw University.

Dr. Sesay was and still is a colleague, a friend, a mentor, a scholar of high caliber, and one of the handful Administrators who take whatever they do beyond the call of duty. I know he has big dreams for his students in the Department of Education. But he also continues to lend a helping hand to students majoring in Liberal Studies, which is a program I have been coordinating for the past few years in the Department of Humanities. The Shaw University Liberal Studies Program is Dr. Sesay's "baby", and it will one day grow into a Master's Program. Not a single week has gone by without him sending me such words of encouragement and prophesy, and I do take them very seriously.

In a nutshell, I recommend Dr. Sesay for promotion to the rank of Professor. He is a rare find, and there is no doubt in my mind that he deserves it very much indeed.

Sincerely,

Désiré Baloubi

Désiré Baloubi, Ph.D.
Associate Professor of English and Linguistics
Department of Humanities
Shaw University
(919) 546-8307

Comment:
*It's really heartwarming
to hear this, especially
from a sound scholar and
colleague.*

Thanks, my friend.

SHAW UNIVERSITY

March 27, 2006

Faculty Development Advisory Committee (FDAC):

RE: Letter of Recommendation for Dr. Allyson Sesay

I have known Dr. Allyson Sesay since January 7, 2005 when I joined the Department of Education at Shaw University. During this short period, I have known him as a highly knowledgeable, dedicated, and committed facilitator of learning who is highly skilled in student development. Dr. Sesay is a caring professional educator that understands how to motivate students.

He is a resourceful, creative, and goal oriented person who is willing to serve this great institution and the community. He is highly respected by students and faculty members in the department as a person with great knowledge and skills.

Based on my experience teaching and working with him in the department, and serving in many committees, I can unreservedly recommend Dr. Allyson Sesay for the Faculty Award for Teaching Excellence. For further information, I can be reached at (919) 546-8539.

Sincerely

Comfort O. Okpala, Ed.D.
Assistant Professor & Coordinator of Research and Assessment
Department of Education
Shaw University
Raleigh, North Carolina

Comment:
*Thanks for the collegiality.
I appreciate it.*

UNIVERSITY

November 7, 2007

Dr. Delores Jerman
Chairperson of the Department of Education
Shaw University

RE: A Letter of Recommendation for Dr. Allyson Sesay

Dear Dr. Jerman,

It is with honor and pleasure that I write this recommendation letter for Dr. Allyson A. Sesay in support of his application for promotion from the rank of Associate Professor to Professor at Shaw University. As the Director of Faculty Development at Shaw University, and a Co-Principal Investigator on a grant proposal we jointly wrote to the Department of Education, I have worked closely with and observed him over the past four years, and I believe I can adequately evaluate him.

Dr. Allyson Sesay has twenty-four years of consistent professional teaching experience at the high school and college levels. He joined the Shaw University Faculty in 1997 bringing with him unparalleled dedication to student learning, his enthusiasm about education, and his love for people in general. At Shaw University, he has proven himself to be an engaged scholar with demonstrated productivity in the areas of teaching, research, and service. His work ethics as a scholar and campus leader has earned him great respect from his students and colleagues. While Chair of the Faculty Development Advisory Committee (August 2003-August 2007), which is charged with evaluating proposals for the mini-grant awards and portfolios for the University Award for Teaching Excellence, I was privy to how well the other constituents of the university think of Dr. Sesay. Among his colleagues, he is described as one of the most scholarly faculty on campus, who has provided knowledge, motivation, and leadership to others through his several presentations at national conferences and at Shaw University. His students characterize him as not only an excellent teacher and mentor, but also as someone whose role is often transformed into that of a motivator and a counselor, providing them with guidance. Dr. Sesay has the ability to effectively convey information that generates critical and analytical thinking, as well as thought-provocating discussions.

I can attest to his very keen interest in continuous professional growth, research, excellence in teaching, enhancement of student learning, and multicultural issues. His record of grantsmanship includes two projects funded by the Faculty Development Program at Shaw University over the period of four years. This speaks to his relentless pursuit of excellence in teaching, and scholarship. Data obtained from his research have been presented at Shaw University and at national conferences. His research projects have had a positive impact on the viability and visibility of Shaw University. The results have been used to design new strategies (published in handbooks) for effective advising of students in order to increase student retention and graduation rates. All of his presentations on academic advising, pedagogical issues, and multiculturalism are published in different conference proceedings.

Department Natural Sciences & Mathematics

Dr. Sesay is a very resourceful, creative, and goal-oriented person who has willingly given of himself to serve Shaw University and the community at large. His willingness to go beyond the "call of duty" has led him to be a member of several campus committees and assume numerous leadership roles. This is further evidenced by: (1) his research agenda, culminating in several conference presentations; (2) program development – he conceptualized, developed, and implemented the Multi-disciplinary Studies Program at Shaw University and chaired the department for three years; (3) proposal development initiatives. These activities have earned him a distinguished record in the areas of research, teaching, and service. His love of children and his drive to positively impact their lives have been the driving force behind his tremendous involvement in the Wake County Public School System. He has and continues to serve on several campus committees. In his department he serves on the: Curriculum Committee; Syllabus Committee; and the Peer Review Committee; and institutionally, he is a member of the Strategic Planning Committee. As a result of his outstanding record of teaching and service to the University and its community, Dr. Sesay was the first-place recipient of the 2006 University Award for Teaching Excellence.

Recognized several times in the Who's Who Among America's Teachers, respected by his students and colleagues, and having demonstrated an outstanding record of accomplishment in the areas of teaching, scholarship, and service to the University and the community, I therefore recommend Dr. Sesay for promotion to the rank of Professor and without any reservations. Please do not hesitate to contact me if I can be of any further help.

Sincerely,

Grace M. Ndip, PhD
Chairperson
Department of Natural Sciences and Mathematics
Shaw University.

Comment: *I'm really flattered, Dr. Ndip, but thanks, anyway.*

Dr. Sam, *9/18/09*

Thank you for being such a good friend and such a great mentor

Best,
D. Baloubi

THE AFRICA WE KNOW

Reading and Writing Across Disciplines in African and Liberal Studies Programs

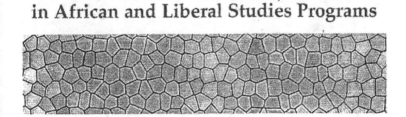

Edited by
Désiré Baloubi, Ph.D.

Comment: *Thanks, my friend, it was a pleasure that I was able to inspire a young colleague who has made tremendous progress in academe as a teacher and scholar since he joined the faculty here at Shaw University.*

INCOMES FROM ADMINISTRATORS

SHAW UNIVERSITY

College of Graduate Studies and
Professional Studies

MEMORANDUM

TO: The Faculty Development Advisory Committee

FROM: Joan D. Barrax
Dean, College of Graduate and Professional Studies

RE: Faculty Award for Teaching Excellence

DATE: March 29, 2006

I am pleased to write a letter of endorsement for Dr. Allyson Sesay, a faculty member in the Department of Education who is noteworthy for his teaching excellence, scholarship, and service.

Over the past three years that I've known Dr. Sesay, he has received outstanding peer and student evaluations for his performance as a classroom teacher. For instance, in the past year, 100% of a class of 25 agreed or strongly agreed that he demonstrated knowledge of the subject matter, showed practical application of the content, made effective uses of aids, assigned relevant reading, showed respect for students, was punctual, and used appropriate methods of evaluation. More than 95% agreed or strongly agreed that he effectively organized the content of the material, returned graded material in timely fashion, was available for consultation, increased their interest in the subject, presented new viewpoints or ideas regarding the subject matter, and inspired confidence in the field. Indeed, Dr. Sesay was recognized three times in Who's Who Among America's Teachers.

Dr. Sesay constantly seeks to improve himself as a faculty member, attending training sessions and workshops, for example on the use of PowerPoint, Blackboard, academic advising, proposal writing, videoconferencing, and culturally relevant pedagogy. In addition, Dr. Sesay is also one of the most scholarly faculty members at Shaw University, having made/had accepted 12 presentations at national conferences. He is currently working on two books for publication, one on educational research for beginners and the other on "Teaching Tips for Student Teachers and Beginning Teachers."

As a faculty member, Dr. Sesay also provides service to the University and to the public schools. He currently serves as a member of the University's Strategic Planning Committee; advisor to the International Students Association; and member of the Department of Education's Curriculum Committee, Syllabus Committee, and Graduate Program Committee. He has provided multicultural education workshops to partner public schools and a presentation on "How to Prepare for Job Interviews" for Communities in Schools. He has served as a mentor at Conn Elementary School and is currently recruiting faculty to volunteer at SPARC Academy. He is also developing a proposal for a comparative look at "Women in Academics" in Africa.

In summary, Dr. Sesay's record of teaching, scholarship, and service highly qualifies him to be recognized for his performance as a faculty member.

Cc: Dr. Deloris Jerman

Celebrating Excellence Since 1865

118 East South Street •Raleigh, North Carolina 27601 • 919-719-1995 • FAX 919-743-5702 • 919-546-8531

Comment: *It's really uplifting to hear this from a very demanding boss and very tough job performance evaluator*

THE RENAISSANCE YEARS

AT

SHAW UNIVERSITY

TALBERT O. SHAW, PH.D.

— 1987-2002 —

8' May, 2008

To Dr. Sesay,

Thank you for excellent service to Shaw University. I personally thank you for being such a positive force in the Department of Education. May your activities bring many new successes and blessings.

President Emeritus

Comment: *It is really gratifying to have been thought of so highly by such an accomplished academic and highly successful administrator in the U.S. higher education. I am happy I was able to contribute my share in your distinguished service at Shaw University*

200

SHAW UNIVERSITY

MEMORANDUM

TO: Dr. Ademola Ejire, Chair, Promotion Committee
       Professor, Department of Natural Sciences and Mathematics

       Dr. K. P. Satagopan, Promotion Committee
       Professor, Department of Natural Sciences and Mathematics

       Dr. Elvira Williams, Promotion Committee
       Professor and Dean, College of Arts and Sciences

FROM: Dr. Deloris L. Jerman
       Assistant Dean, College of Graduate and Professional Studies/
       Chair, Department of Education

DATE: November 14, 2007

RE: Dr. Allyson Sesay's Request for Academic Promotion to the Rank of Professor

Thank you for agreeing to serve on the Promotion Committee to review Dr. Allyson
Sesay's request for academic promotion to the rank of Professor. Dr. Allyson Sesay,
Associate Professor in the Department of Education, is a distinguished faculty member
who has demonstrated excellence in the teaching profession, the scholarship of teaching,
and has shown an outstanding commitment and dedication to student learning. For these
reasons and the ones listed below, I am pleased to have the opportunity to write a letter of
recommendation for Dr. Sesay.

Dr. Sesay has a Bachelor of Science in Agricultural Economics (Langston University,
1976), Master of Education in Foundations of Education/Comparative Education
(University of Illinois at Urbana, 1978), and a Doctor of Philosophy in Educational
Policy Analysis (University of Illinois at Urbana, 1981). Dr. Sesay has taught in higher
education for twenty-three years and was promoted to the rank of Associate Professor in
1990 at the University of Maine and maintained that rank upon coming to Shaw
University in 1997. Between 1999 and 2002, Dr. Sesay served as the Chair of the
Department of Multidisciplinary Studies at Shaw University. Since that time he has
worked in the Department of Education and currently serves as the Coordinator of
Academic Advisement and Volunteer Service. In addition to teaching and advising
assigned advisees, he is responsible for coordinating and conducting academic advising
meetings for all Education majors each semester, providing orientation and mentoring to
new faculty members, and conducting research in order to write/evaluate the
Department's Plan of Collaboration with the Public Schools, as required by the North
Carolina Department of Public Instruction.

Celebrating Excellence since 1111

201

He is recognized as an outstanding teacher by students, peers in his Department and across campus, and in P-12 schools. During the past several years, he has taught such undergraduate courses as EDU 111: Foundations of Education, EDU 415: Tests and Measurements, EBK 385: Multicultural Education in the B-K Classroom, and EDU 319: Graduate Support - Educational Research. Graduate courses that he has taught include ECI 640: Historical, Philosophical, and Social Foundations of American Education; ECI 643: Social and Political Problems in Education; and ECI 634: Multicultural Education – Planning and Implementing Instruction for Diverse Learners. Departmental faculty members, including Dr. Sesay, updated syllabi and developed and used common rubrics to assess students' work in LiveText each semester since 2003. Dr. Sesay participated in the University's first offering of courses via videoconference/broadcast to students at several CAPE centers across North Carolina in 2003. In summer 2007, he developed an online course that he taught in fall 2007. Additionally, he offered another course online during the fall and is developing an online course for spring 2008. Dr. Sesay's teaching reflects the unit's conceptual framework (teaching that encourages students' development of reflection, critical-thinking and problem-solving skills, and professional dispositions), research, theories, and current developments in his field of teaching. He integrates diversity and the use of instructional technology throughout course work. He uses a variety of instructional strategies that reflect an understanding of different learning styles and adjusts instruction appropriately to enhance candidate learning. Because he understands assessment technology, he uses multiple forms of assessment in determining his effectiveness, and uses the data to improve his practice. Dr. Sesay has developed relationships, programs, and projects with colleagues and faculty in other units of the University to develop and refine knowledge bases, conduct research, make presentations, and improve the quality of education for all students. Results of student evaluations consistently show that Dr. Sesay exemplifies the evaluation criteria. In the Department of Education, multiple assessments are used to assess faculty performance. Overall, evaluation results of Dr. Sesay's performance on the Individual Annual Review and Evaluation (IARE), Peer Evaluations, and the Shaw University Employee Performance Appraisal Report were at the target/superior level. In 2006, he received the Shaw University Teaching Excellence Award.

Dr. Sesay demonstrates scholarly work related to teaching, learning, and his field of specialization. In addition to providing leadership in the profession, schools, and professional associations at state, national, and international levels, he has a strong record as a researcher. He has published at least 16 articles, contributed a chapter to a book, and written at least 12 unpublished manuscripts. Three articles have been submitted for publication in 2007. Other recognitions include receiving research grants from Shaw University's Faculty Development Program in 2003-2004 and 2004-2005 and being named to *Who's Who Among America's Teachers* for 2002, 2004, 2005, and 2006. Additionally, he has served as an invited lecturer, presenting seminars and workshops and making presentations at local, state, and national conferences, and in the public schools. Areas of research interest include policy research—analysis of educational policy formulation, implementation, and policy impact; international comparisons of children and youths' educational and occupational aspirations; and multicultural education and diversity issues. The following book projects are underway: (1) a comprehensive text in teacher education, (2) a book on pedagogy for the student teacher and beginning teacher, and (3) a book on educational research for the beginning researcher. To stay abreast of current issues and trends in education, Dr. Sesay holds membership in professional associations in his field, such as Phi Delta Kappa (PDK), the National Academic Advising Association (NACADA), the National Association for Multicultural Education (NAME), the Comparative and International Education Society (CIES), and the Association of Third World Studies (ATWS).

In addition to teaching and scholarship, Dr. Sesay monitors and documents the service of the Department to the public schools. He provided service to the University and the community by developing and presenting a PowerPoint presentation that was used in the Career Fair of Majors (part of the Freshman Studies Program), provided service to the public schools by tutoring/mentoring a student at a local elementary school, and designed a multicultural education workshop and invited beginning teachers from the public schools. Further, Dr. Sesay has served/serves on numerous University committees, including the Strategic Planning Committee, the Faculty Development Advisory Committee, the Subcommittee of the Inauguration Committee for the inauguration of the University's 13th President, and the Administrative Subcommittee for the Southern Association of Colleges and Schools (SACS) re-accreditation visit in 2002. In the Department of Education, he serves on the Peer Review Committee, the Curriculum Committee, the Graduate Program Committee, and the Teacher Education Council (TEC). He also serves on the College of Graduate and Professional Studies Grievance Committee.

Much more could be written about Dr. Sesay's work at Shaw University. He is truly a role model for us all. His accomplishments are numerous, as evidenced in his portfolio. After reviewing his portfolio, I feel you will agree that he is the perfect candidate for academic promotion to the rank of Professor. I am submitting three copies each of this memorandum and Dr. Sesay's portfolio for review to Dr. Ejire, the Promotion Committee Chair, for appropriate distribution. Again, thank you for serving on Dr. Sesay's promotion committee.

November 14, 2007   3

Comment: *Thanks, Dr. Jerman, for such a powerful recommendation. It's really uplifting to have such a recommendation from someone like you who is fair and uncompromising in performance appraisal.*

CHAPTER 10

Some Personal Perspectives
and General Conclusion

In this chapter my objective is two-fold: First, I want to discuss a few selected aspects of Shaw University's programs and services and express my concern about the direction the institution is heading as it continues to pursue its motto of "Strides to Excellence: Only the Best." Second, I want to suggest some actions for the university to at least try. These actions, I believe, have potentially positive outcomes for sustained development in our increasingly competitive higher education marketplace. The aspects of the university I have selected to address are as follows: appointment and promotion to key positions, employee compensation and employee morale. I'll also take on a somehow controversial question "what does student success really mean?" After these discussions, I will present my general conclusion which will bring the book to a close.

Appointment and Promotion to Key Positions

During my years of sojourning at Shaw University, I have observed with dismay how some appointments and promotions have been made to some key positions including the highest office of the president, vice president, deans, departmental chairs, and director of programs. Some of the decisions to appoint and promote have not been transparent, to say the least, even where there are stipulated guidelines for reaching such decisions. The faculty, for example, need to be fully involved in the appointment of persons who will have significant power and authority to shape the future of the institution. It cannot be overemphasized the very negative and sometimes disastrous and far-reaching consequences the appointment of an inept, incompetent, corrupt, or overly authoritarian administrator can have on an institution. One important situation to be guarded against is the appointment of persons of lower academic rank to lead colleagues of much higher rank and work experience. For example, such appointments to positions of dean or departmental chair can create some serious moral problem, some of which, though they may not be manifested openly, can, nevertheless, negatively impact the work ethic among the faculty. Sometimes the junior colleague is unilaterally promoted as a way of narrowing the gap in faculty rank. For example, an Assistant Professor is appointed dean or departmental chair and then automatically promoted to the rank of an Associate Professor so as to give "legitimacy" to the chair or dean position. I have seen this happen at Shaw University more than once, and it affected faculty morale significantly. On one occasion, it even led to the resignation of a very seasoned faculty member, which was a big loss to the affected department and faculty. The fact that promotions result in increased salaries and prestige, too, make this a very thorny and sensitive matter. There is nothing wrong with giving a young and uprising academic a chance to fast track to positions of authority and eminence; however, this should never be done at the expense of eroding employee morale and the concomitant effect of compromising the smooth and efficient running of the organization or unit.

Employee Compensation

A key factor that can destroy an organization is the unfair method of compensation of its employees. All things being equal, the level of qualification (degrees, years of experience, productivity, etc.) should be positively related to amount of income. What a shame it is to have professors with terminal degrees and several years of experience earning

205

sometimes 10 to 15 percent less salary than a staff with only a bachelor's degree or associate degree, or less than another academic colleague who completed their terminal degree only a few years back! Though some will argue that this practice goes on in institutions across the country, this does not however make it right, and it should not be encouraged at Shaw University, which professes to distinguish itself as a fertile training ground for the moral and ethical nurturing of its students. Let's put into practice and live by the dictate of our motto *Pro Christo et Humanitate* meaning "For Christ and Humanity."

Employee Morale

If there is anything that can glue the relationship among the employees of an organization, I do not thing there can be any factor more powerful than good employee morale. During my 15-year sojourn at Shaw University, I served under the administrations of four presidents – first, the presidency of Dr. Talbert O. Shaw who was on site when I first arrived in 1997; then came, in order, Dr. Clarence Newsome; Dr. Dorothy Cowser Yancy; followed by Dr. Irma McClaurin whose administration lasted for only one academic year, and then again Dr. Yancy, who returned in August of 2011. I observed and personally experienced varying levels of employee morale during each of these four administrations. What I want to do here is to give my personal impressions of employee morale during these periods.

In my opinion, if one could chart or graph employee morale during the tenures of the four presidents mentioned above, the resulting graph would resemble a parabola of upward and downward swings or trends. In my personal opinion, faculty moral was at its highest at Shaw University during the tenure of Dr. Talbert O. Shaw. He was not perfect by any means: there were times when he was autocratic in order to get things done, and that understandably, angered some employees, including some members of the faculty. However, he had a great vision when he came in 1987 as the university's 12th president. Indeed, he was a kind of messiah to rescue the university from an impending financial collapse. It was a challenge many administrators would not have taken, but he did, and in a matter of a few years, he got Shaw University in the print of the electronic media with very positive publicity, contrary to the negative publicity from prophets and prophetesses of doom at the time. The university started meeting its financial obligations, especially that of employee salaries. Timely payment of salaries and yearly across-the-board bonuses became the rule rather than the exception. We looked forward to the end of year Christmas social at the Student Union Building. The increase in salary paid in December was made retroactive to July, and so we received a backlog in arrears of five months. That made the take-home package for December, paid before the Christmas vacation, quite a big bundle. We went on holidays with a sweet frame of mind to return the following January to start the spring semester with a renewed energy and enthusiasm to continue pursuant of our motto "Strides to excellence: Why not the best." Yes, those were the good old days at Shaw University, days when the expression *Shaw Family* really made a lot of sense.

With the exit of President Shaw at his volition, it must be emphasized, came President Clarence Newsom and his team of administrators, most of them from Washington, DC. Dr. Newsome came from the Divinity School at Howard University, the same institution from which his predecessor had come.

President Shaw left Shaw University in sound financial health with a sizable endowment. The Newsome administrative team consisted of *heavy spenders*. Capital projects, including renovation of buildings, updating of the institution's technology infrastructures, and others soon ate up the institution's endowment. Borrowing from the local financial institutions to meet basic running costs became the norm. To keep the institution afloat, university properties were offered as collateral to secure loans. Salary disparities, especially between the administration's team members and their "favorites", and the rest of the university particularly the faculty were glaring and, understandably, did not auger well for boosting employee morale. Therefore, unlike the Shaw administration, which ended on a high note, that of Dr. Newsome had to end on a bad note with the Board of Trustees, to put it mildly. I do not remember a sendoff party for Dr. Newsome and his team like the one given for Dr. Shaw.

Dr. Dorothy Cowser Yancy was appointed interim President, the first female to serve in that capacity in the university's 144 years of existence at the time. She was brought in to kind of lift Shaw University from a huge and deep financial hole. With a track record as a great fund raiser and an astute leader in higher education, Dr. Yancy in short order created positive signs of recovery from a glaring downward spiral in the university's financial posture. A cover story of the September/October 2009 Spectacular Magazine noted:

> Living up to her reputation, she hit the ground running, by immediately reviewing the University's academic programs and analyzing the financial state of the school, in an effort to determine the best possible course of action for eliminating debt and raising the money necessary to take the University into the future (p.11).

This veteran higher education administrator promised to adopt new and innovative strategies to move the institution to a new height but warned that "these new strategies will obviously mean that the ship must be run much tighter and where necessary, we must cut back" (p.11). She put words into action, and after only a year at Shaw University the faculty and staff held a grand *Appreciation Day* in her honor. The following are a few of the proclamations made at the ceremony in appreciation of the positive impact she had made at the university after only a year:

WHEREAS, Shaw University, now in its 145th year of operation, has a rich history of "providing educational opportunities for a diverse population who otherwise might not have the opportunity for education: (University Mission), our rich heritage points to the strong leadership of remarkable persons, such as Dr. Dorothy Cowser Yancy, the current Interim President of Shaw University.

WHEREAS, an individual who performs at an exceptional level in an organization should be recognized and acknowledged, this proclamation formally and publicly affirms the many accomplishments of our Interim President, Dr. Yancy.

WHEREAS, under the leadership of Dr. Yancy, a manageable level of fiscal strength and stability have been restored at Shaw University.

WHEREAS, Dr. Yancy arranged the repackaging of the Shaw University's $31M debt such that five (5) buildings and their appurtenances were used as collateral, instead of over fifty (50) buildings and appurtenances on and off the main campus.

WHEREAS, Dr. Yancy improved the institution's financial ratios, restricted the leadership team, and identified more faculty to take leadership roles in preparation for SACS reaffirmation in 2012.

WHEREAS, Dr. Yancy implemented a plan for extensive renovation of buildings, thereby, completing deferred maintenance on a total of seventeen (17) buildings on the main campus and at CAPE sites.

WHEREAS, Dr. Yancy improved faculty morale by attending faculty meetings and providing updates on the state of Shaw University, establishing the Leon Riddick Faculty/Staff Dining Room, and holding the first ever Faculty/Staff Appreciation Cookout.

These proclamations speak volumes for someone who had been at the university for only one academic year. Importantly also, the students were excited about the changes President Yancy had brought to the university.

In the cover story cited earlier, a senior Theatre major was quoted as saying that since Dr. Yancy had arrived at Shaw University, "the overall atmosphere has changed for the better"(p.11). Many other returning students were said to have echoed the same and similar compliments, to which I do personally subscribe.

On Student Success

I have had for a long time debated within myself and colleagues in academe the question of the meaning of student success. I have been surprised as well as amazed at how these colleagues have perceived student success. For example, at one of our Strategic Planning Committee meeting at the university, one colleague asked in a rather angry and condescending voice "What's the point when you find our graduates working at Wal-Mart and Food Lion?" Wal-Mart is America's biggest retail chains, and Food Lion is a big grocery enterprise with several branches across the country. Another colleague, also in a condescending and cynical manner, remarked to me about one his former students [a Shaw University graduate] as follows: "I saw one of my former students working as a cashier at K-Mart and she tried to hide from me. I said to myself, where do you think I will expect to find you working?" By implication, these two learned colleagues of mine were saying those graduates who picked up employment at retail stores like Wal-Mart and K-Mart and at a grocery store like Food Lion were, in essence, "failures" or unsuccessful. They were the weak students who graduated not *cum laude* but as one commencement guest speaker at the university humorously put it *"thank God laude,"* meaning that they barely made it out of college (i.e., with low GPAs of 2.00 and thereabout). My colleagues were implying that these graduates will not do much in life socioeconomically. Well, I have a word for these colleagues and others with the same or similar mindset. These graduates can do well in life and become important contributors to the development of their communities, state and the nation. I will return to this point later.

How an institution perceives student success will to a large extent influence how it organizes and delivers its programs to achieve its professed mission statement. This will in turn influence the type and quality of academic advisement services the institution provides its students. A cursory examination of the mission statements of many, if not all, colleges and universities across the nation will reveal an espoused commitment to prepare students who will have acquired the cultural competence to function effectively in a diverse and interdependent world. These are great mission statements to say the least. However, I have always been concerned about the match between such pronouncements in an institution's mission statement and what is actually practiced, vis-à-vis preparing students for success after graduation. I contend that colleges and universities, actively or passively, tend to focus a little too much attention on the aspect of their mission that deals with the preparation of students for graduate work and the world of work. Teaching and learning, including academic advising activities, thus seem to revolve around improving retention and graduation rates and on increasing students' chances to pursue graduate studies upon completion of their undergraduate programs. Accreditation agencies such as the National Association for the Accreditation of Teacher Education (NCATE), regional accreditation bodies such as the Southern Association of Colleges and Schools (SACS), and various state departments of public instruction use these student outcomes as important criteria or benchmarks in their evaluation of institutions for accreditation and re-affirmation of accreditation. The fact that these outcomes are easier to be documented quantitatively makes them more appealing than student outcomes such as good citizenship, cultural sensitivity, and good character which are as critically important as preparation for careers in an institution's mission and vision statements.

A major consequence of an institution's preoccupation with achieving the student outcomes alluded to above is a focus on recruiting and retaining those high-achieving students who are expected to achieve "success" and thereby enhance the institution's image and reputation. I am talking here of those student who graduated with honors – the *summa cum laudes, magna cum laudes* and *cum laudes*. Let me hasten to emphasize the point that I see nothing wrong with any institution making desperate efforts and committing large sums of money to attract and graduate this caliber of students. My concern is what we do to help those underprepared students we recruit into our institutions where they sometimes feel neglected and undervalued. This discussion focuses on those students who one commencement speaker at Shaw University characterized as graduates in the category "Thank God laude" – that is, those who barely made it to graduation – those with 2.00 and low 2.00 GPAs. These are the students the university would prefer to keep away from members of visiting accreditation teams for fear that they would not represent the caliber of students the institution claims to produce. I want to present in the next few pages an honest and down-to-earth discussion of the meaning of *student success*, and more importantly, how to effectively prepare this often underserved student population so that they can become productive and personally-fulfilled members of society. Even though they may not go on to graduate and professional school, as in the case with some of Shaw University's graduates, they will, nevertheless, become citizens with characteristics such as these, among others:

- Law-abiders (A person is most free who is law-abiding).
- Role models for persons, especially at-risk children and youths, in their communities.
- Better and more responsible parents who will be more supportive of efforts to educate their children. For example, they can help with homework and participate comfortably and actively in Parent Teachers' Association meetings.
- Persons with political savvy. They can discuss political issues more intelligently, exercise their right to vote, and also importantly mobilize campaigns to encourage others to take advantage of this right.
- Wiser consumers of goods and services.

  - Know how to better negotiate for the purchase of goods such as a home, a car – areas in which uninformed and unsophisticated consumers are taken advantage of (taken to the cleaners, as the expression goes).

- Prudent managers of their finances

  - Know how to budget, how to use credit cards wisely, and how to avoid conspicuous consumption (buying stuff not necessarily needed but because their neighbor has them).

I make these points because the Shaw University's second semester Freshman Studies course provides instruction on these practical life skills mentioned above. In fact, I have taught this course myself and am therefore very familiar with the student learning outcomes addressed and the methodology employed in this regard.

The list of empowerments that all Shaw students have the opportunity to develop goes on:

- Organize community development activities such as voter registration, adult literacy programs, good health promotion campaigns, and the like.
- Contributors to the economy by paying taxes rather than living on welfare. This is referred to as the social rate of return to education.
- Enjoyers of worthwhile, stress-free leisure.

I hope that we in academe – faculty, staff and administrators alike - will ponder this question of what *student success* truly means and that we will begin to pay greater attention to helping those students who may very likely not qualify to gain acceptance into graduate and professional schools, or to high profile positions in the private or public sector, but who can, nevertheless, become productive members of their communities and the world. Just maybe, accrediting bodies as well as state and federal governments will start reconsidering their perception of student success as they increasingly tie funding and faculty compensation to student learning outcomes and become aware that student learning outcomes cannot be limited to going to graduate school or securing a white-color job in the public or private sector.

Concluding Remarks

My sojourning in the Shaw University's vineyard for fifteen years was filled with a variety of professional career and personal life experiences which will remain indelible in my mind. Because the impetus for writing was largely to preserve those experiences, this book is in effect a memoir of my professional career, much of which was spent at Shaw University. I also had an eight-year sojourn at Usmanu Danfodio University in Sokoto, Nigeria. Perhaps I shall write in the future about the variety of rich academic and socio-cultural experiences I had there. I did learn there that I may have lost opportunities there, opportunities I was resolved to not let slip at Shaw.

In my 15-year tenure at Shaw University, the first HBCU in the Southern United States of America, and the mother of several other institutions of higher learning in North Carolina, I carried out my tripartite role as teacher, researcher and community service provider with enthusiasm and an unwavering commitment to contribute to the promotion of the institution's motto, "strides to excellence only the best." In the process I met several faculty colleagues whose friendship I will cherish for life. This book has been about my tripartite collaborative efforts with these colleagues as well as with my students and community members.

One arm of my work has been research, mostly what is called action research geared to specific problems and finding ways to improve practice – particularly, teaching and academic advising, taking due cognizance of the impact of multiculturalism.

A second arm was academic advising, which developmental advising experts rightly consider a form of teaching. I devoted three chapters to that important subject. I explored students' perception of the concept of academic advising and their relationships with their academic advisors. All categories of students require sound academic advising to enhance their chances of persistence and graduation, but there are some special populations of students who need special attention to ensure their academic success. Student-athletes comprise one of these special populations, and a chapter was devoted to address the challenges these students face in their efforts to combine academics and athletics. Coaches, professors, staff, and administrators all have important roles to play in ensuring the success of student-athletes in school and upon graduation. Research has shown that few become professional athletes. Securing a sound education, therefore, is of critical importance to their futures.

Sometimes, the little things we as instructors and academic advisors say and do to our students, seemingly trivial, can have significant impact on their academic and personal development. A chapter of the book is devoted to a personal experience with an advisee of mine in this connection.

Another chapter dealt with traditional vs. nontraditional students. It takes a special kind of teacher to be able to effectively engage both kinds in collaborative learning modes so that both can experience success. My research revealed that traditional and non-traditional students preferred to take classes together because of the mutual benefits they can derive from such an experience.

Reflecting on my personal experiences as the only Black professor in an overwhelming White university, I explored the experiences of White students as a minority group studying in a predominantly Black institution. Except for a few uncomfortable experiences, the White students found it a very worthwhile academic and cultural learning experience to study and live in an environment where they were a minority group. Much credit goes to Shaw University for providing a conducive environment that facilitated such a culturally pluralistic living and learning experience.

The chapter reporting on experiences of women faculty reflected the general situation of inequity they face in their efforts to advance their careers in the ivory tower. Inequity was reported in the assignment of workload (curricular and extra-curricular), salary, and lack of mentorship, among others. However, Shaw University has made some significant improvements in providing gender equity. For example, it has appointed women to key administrative positions. At the time I conducted the study on females at the university, four out of the six members of the executive leadership and cabinets were women. These included the president, the first ever in the institution's 144 years of existence at the time.

It would be remiss of me not to mention two more groups. I want to give special recognition to male colleagues at Shaw for their support and genuine friendship. And, of course the group that I cherished most during my sojourning at the university was my students. In the preceding chapter, I documented a variety of what I termed psychic incomes that I acquired from my relationships with students as well as faculty colleagues and administrators.

Shaw University has gone through trying times since its founding in 1865, many of them financial, which had resulted in the closure of some of its unique programs including its 4-year medical program, the first in the nation. There were times when the institution came almost to the brink of extinction, but it always found a way to survive. I believe without question that Shaw University's doors will remain open to continue to provide a sound education to a diverse body of students from within the United States of America and beyond. God bless Shaw University.

Printed in the United States
By Bookmasters